THE FAST

Rediscovering Jesus' Pathway to Power

Lou Engle

ISBN 978-1-7343823-0-3

Library of Congress Control Number: 2019957230

Engle House Publishing
102 S Tejon St. STE 1100
Colorado Springs, CO 80903

CONTENTS

DEDICATION

I dedicate this book to all my children, who have done extended fasts and rejoiced in their father's calling. May you carry on the legacy of many generations who sought God in this ancient path of holy pursuit. May your children and your children's children rise up and fast and pray that the God of my fathers would ever be their God!

INTRODUCTION

Decades ago, I received a book called *Shaping History Through Prayer and Fasting* by Derek Prince. That book became the textbook of my life. The basic premise and biblical revelation of that book is that the future of nations is shaped by the united prayers and fastings of God's people. Thirty-five years after reading this book, we are calling the globe to united prayer and fasting, believing that the earth will yield its harvest. Before Derek Prince died, a friend of mine spoke to him and asked about his legacy. Prince mentioned the significance of "TheCall." When I heard those words, I began to weep and said to the Lord, "If you will allow me, I will take Derek Prince's seed to the ends of the earth." This book is part of my obedience to that divine invitation. The Church worldwide is entering a time of a global reenactment of Jesus' extended fasting for a global Jesus harvest. The ancient tools of intercession are being recovered and the spiritually violent are taking the kingdom by force.

This book is a book of dreams, of divine photos. I'm unapologetic in writing it. Years ago I was wrestling with the question of whether or not I should share my dreams and prophetic stories for fear of pride. I strongly sensed the Lord speaking to me, "If you don't tell the stories, you will never see movements come forth." God asked Ezekiel, "What do you see?" Ezekiel saw a valley of dry bones. God said, "Prophesy to the bones to live again." Ezekiel prophesied and bones began to rattle. Ezekiel first saw a spiritual vision, then he spoke and movement took place. I have seen dreams and I write them down so that those who read them may run on the pathway and destination to which the dreams point. I hear the bones of an ancient army rattling once again. They are on an ancient, fasting pathway to power.

Abraham Heschel said, "More is learned in one moment of awe than in a lifetime of calculation." In this light, I appeal to you to read these stories and dreams. Unshackle yourself from the chains of unbiblical rationality and allow yourself to experience a measure of awe of the God who speaks. Like Jacob, when he had a dream, let us say, "How awesome is this place! This is none other than the gate of heaven and the house of God!" We need an Awe-Wakening. Judge these words you read to see if they align with Scripture and if they witness to your spirit. If they do, then renounce a casual approach to the prophetic. If you find yourself stirred by these stories, move beyond awe to action. Live the Jesus Fast. Step into a lifelong adventure of liberating flight and revelation by fasting forward into a new era in your life and for the world.

CHAPTER 1

A CALL TO FASTING

Every prophet has to come from civilization, but every prophet has to go into the wilderness. He must have a strong impression of a complex society and all that it has to give, and then he must serve periods of isolation and meditation. This is the process by which psychic dynamite is made.

Winston Churchill

"A man can receive nothing unless it has been given to him from heaven . . . He must increase, but I must decrease." (John 3:27, 30) These were the roaring words of John the Baptist when challenged by his disciples regarding the ministry of Jesus surpassing his own.

Even at the beginning of 2019, this scripture exploded in my spirit. I was on a forty-day season of fasting, drinking coffee in a coffee shop. Obviously, I was calling coffee "brown water"! I read that morning that the season of Lent is actually a time to humble oneself and return to the power and victory of Jesus' forty-day fast in the wilderness. I felt the Holy Spirit speak to me, "Call Europe to a forty-day Lent fast in 2020, March 1 through April 9." Actually, in a few minutes I was going to make a phone call to European leaders to ask them if they would mobilize a forty-day fast for the harvest of Europe.

As I was walking out of the coffee shop to make that phone call, I noticed a woman reading a book. I passed by her, went outside, and instantly was stopped in my tracks by the Holy Spirit saying, "Turn around and find out what book that lady is reading." Immediately, I turned around, re-entered the coffee shop, and humbly asked the woman, "Excuse me, ma'am, what book are you reading?" She said, "The title of this book is *Forty Days of Decrease*. It's about the forty-day fast during Lent." I was in shock! I said, "Ma'am, you have no idea how significant this is to me. I'm about to make a phone call to European leaders, calling them into the Lent fast." She said, "Can I pray for you?" There in a common coffee shop she prayed, "Lord, loose the forty-day fast of Lent all throughout Europe and pour out your Spirit on the whole continent in the name of Jesus!"

It is with this word, among many others, that I am urging all nations of the earth to commit to a massive, multiyear pattern of extended fasting for global harvest.

As I look through the rearview mirror of my life journal and journey, I am apprehended with the realization of how forcefully and frequently the forty-day theme of prayer and fasting has presented itself. I have received from heaven, primarily, the call to do and mobilize worldwide extended fasting. I wouldn't have chosen it, but a man can only receive that which has been given to him from above. I must decrease, He must increase.

To read this book is to read a story. Yes, partly my story, but primarily it is the story of Jesus and His original forty-day Jesus Fast that released the original Jesus anointing for evangelism and harvest. It is also a prophetic summons calling for a global reenactment and recovery of Jesus' original pattern and pathway leading to power from on high.

This pattern was revealed in an amazing dream given to a young man the day after Billy Graham, the great evangelist, died. This young man recounted the following.

In the dream, Billy Graham had died and left these words to be read after his passing: "I have hidden a treasure for those who seek to find. The treasure map is in The Book." Knowing "The Book" meant the Bible, I opened my Bible and immediately turned to a treasure map that read, "*Go to the river. Find the strongest, most well-rooted tree. Take forty steps east into the wilderness from the strongest tree. There dig.*"

So, I followed the instructions on the map: I went to the river, found the strongest tree, took forty steps eastward from the tree into the wilderness, and began digging. Six feet down I found a wooden treasure chest that was shaped like a coffin. In the chest was an endless number of sickles. I thought, "A man could spend his entire life giving away these sickles and would never be able to give them all away!" Inscribed into the wood on the inside of the chest were the words, "*The harvest is ripe. Equip the laborers.*"

Then, the dream shifted, and I was taken up above the earth. I saw thousands upon tens-of-thousands of people all over the world finding these same chests with the same contents and the same inscription.

I believe the dream is a true word because the treasure map is found in The Book. Billy Graham is a picture of Jesus, the Great Evangelist. True instructions are actually found in the Bible for how to recover the spiritual authority that Jesus walked in during His evangelistic ministry and how to release a new worldwide explosion of evangelism onto the earth. In the dream, the river must be the Jordan River, where Jesus, the strongest tree, the very Tree of Life, went to be baptized by John. Immediately following His baptism at the Jordan River and hearing the words of His Father: "You are My beloved Son, in whom I am well pleased" (Mark 1:11), Jesus took forty steps into the wilderness and began His forty-day fast. There He dug six feet deep and found a coffin, the picture of the death of His flesh on His forty-day fast, and found the treasure chest of spiritual authority and evangelistic power. Jesus' singular sickle reaped the harvest of the lost sheep of the house of Israel. But now, 2,000 years later, a whole generation, even tens of thousands, will find the treasure map in The Book, the fasting pathway and paradigm that Jesus pioneered.

They are discovering sickles, an anointing to evangelize, and they are going to equip millions to reap the end time harvest.

It is my conviction that the passing of Billy Graham marked a watershed moment in history. From the days of Billy Graham until now, the Kingdom of Heaven is suffering violence and a spiritually violent generation is taking it by force, laying hold of the Jesus Fast for the greatest demonstration of power and love the world has ever seen.

With this faith, I "record the vision and inscribe it on tablets, that the one who reads it may run. 'For the vision is yet for the appointed time; it hastens toward the goal and it will not fail. Though it tarries, wait for it; for it will certainly come, it will not delay'" (Hab. 2:2-3 NASB). The vision God has given me has tarried for twenty-four years since my first forty-day fast in 1996. During that fast, I heard the audible voice of God forcefully speaking to me, "Stretch forth a wakening rod over the earth, will you do that?" I now know that command from heaven was about mobilizing extended fasting all over the earth. So I implore you to judge the prophetic stories in this book to see if they align with Scripture and with the witness of your own spirit according to Paul's words in 1 Thess. 5:19-20, "Do not despise prophecies. Test all things; hold fast what is good." If your spirit witnesses for this, then act with courage and faith with thousands around the world. Enter into seasons of intense, focused fasting and begin to mobilize extended fasting and prayer in your homes, churches, cities, denominations, movements, and nations.

After His forty-day fast, Jesus unrolled the scroll of Isaiah and read,

"The Spirit of the Lord is upon Me, because He has anointed Me to preach the gospel to the poor; He has sent Me to heal the brokenhearted, to proclaim liberty to the captives and recovery of sight to the blind, to set at liberty those who are oppressed; to proclaim the acceptable year of the Lord." Then He closed the book, and gave it back to the attendant and sat down. And the eyes of all who were in the synagogue were fixed on Him. And He began to say to them, "Today this Scripture is fulfilled in your hearing" (Luke 4:18-21).

The scroll of Jesus is being unrolled again before the eyes of the earth through His Body. Christ in us is driving us into His wilderness fast so the whole earth may see once again the full manifestation of Jesus' anointing. If Jesus' fast prepared Him to fulfill the prophecies written about Him in The Book, will not His fast also prepare us to fulfill the prophecies over our lives and succeed? 2 Chron. 20:20 says, "Believe the prophets and you will succeed." The year 2020 has now started. It is time to recover the 20/20 vision for the harvest.

Possibly the most significant awakening to my vocational call of mobilizing extended fasting occurred in January 1999. A leader in Youth With A Mission (YWAM) came to me and asked if I would help him call the Church worldwide to a forty-day fast in the first forty days of 2000. The purpose of the fast was to pray for laborers and contend for the release of a global harvest in the new millennium. At the time, I was very unknown. We were in the infant stages of mobilizing TheCall, a movement of fasting and prayer that began with 400,000 people, primarily young people, gathering in Washington, D.C. in 2000.

So when I was asked to mobilize this fast, I was immediately confronted with the impossibility of the project. However, I had some history in seeing God do some amazing things beyond my expectations, so I inquired of the Lord, "If you want me to mobilize this fast, please have a prophet call me with a dream that I'm flying a plane and dropping an atomic bomb."

Atomic Power

There was a reason for that somewhat strange request. At the time, I was reading a book by Franklin Hall titled *Atomic Power With God Thru Fasting and Prayer*, written in 1946. The book arose from the fervor of hundreds of believers who came together in San Diego from various denominations to hear the teachings of Jesus concerning prayer and fasting. Many of these Christians entered into consecration fasts. Some of these fasts were without food from twenty-one to more than sixty days of continuous duration. They were burdened to see the Lord move in a special way. These and many others wanted to see a worldwide revival for salvation and healing of mankind. The amazing results, as these scores of Christians united in fasting and prayer, were stupendous.

The atomic bomb had just been dropped on August 6, 1945 to Hiroshima, and so in 1946 Franklin Hall made the perceptive comparison that what the atomic bomb was to a normal bomb, extended fasting was to normal prayer.

From those humble beginnings in San Diego, Hall's book began to spread like wildfire. God was breathing on the message. The Spirit was driving His people into the wilderness of extended fasting even as the Spirit drove Jesus into the wilderness to fast for forty days. The divine reenactment was on, for God was preparing to move His people into a new era of outpourings of the Spirit and explosive mass evangelism. Then, suddenly, in 1947, the great healing revivals broke out. T.L. Osborn read *Atomic Power With God Thru Fasting and Prayer* and was stirred to enter into long fasting, which launched him into one of the most remarkable evangelistic careers. Hundreds of thousands attended his crusades. Miraculous healings and deliverances followed. Osborn thanked Hall for his impact through the book, saying, "Our lives have been revolutionized by fasting and prayer." Oral Roberts fasted for seven months in 1947, and then his renowned healing ministry broke out. Hall wrote, "This mighty tide of fasting preceded and was a prelude to the massive evangelistic healing campaigns that began stirring Christendom, in which hundreds and even thousands were converted in a single campaign."

Brethren in North Battleford, Canada, received Hall's book late in 1947. In early 1948, a mighty outpouring of the Spirit broke out after the grace of fasting rested on the community all winter long. These Latter Rain brethren said,

> The truth of fasting was one great contributing factor to the revival
> . . . Previously we had not understood the possibility of long fasts.
> The revival would never have been possible without the restoration
> of this great truth through our good brother Hall.

Do you see the pattern? Massive corporate fasting and prayer breaks out in 1946, continuing for years. Then in response, healing breaks out in 1947. Then revival breaks out in 1948. The great evangelistic ministries of Bill Bright, Billy Graham and many others were birthed in 1948 and 1949. It is my conviction and the very premise of this book that we are entering another historic season like the 1940s and 1950s when global fasting will produce mighty anointed sons and daughters for evangelism and missions. Stadiums will be filled. Every home in the nations will hear the gospel. Miracles in the streets will be commonplace. For such a time as this we live and move and have our being. We have not yet seen the full nuclear power of fasting unleashed in our day.

Yes, the generation of the late 1940s and 1950s saw a reenactment of the original fast of Jesus. The fast was not an anomaly, it was a prototype for the last days generation who, by the Holy Spirit, would be compelled into the wilderness of extended fasting, even forty-day fasts, to bring repentance to the Body of Christ and sweep the skies of demonic interference so that the lost, whose eyes have been blinded by the god of this world, might see the light of the glory of God in the face of Christ.

So, strikingly, a prophet called me the very night of my request, saying he had seen a dream in which I was flying a plane and dropping an atomic bomb. It felt like a bomb went off inside of me that moment, but I knew that dream alone wouldn't mobilize the world.

Soon after the visit from the YWAM leader, a prophet named Paul Cain was coming to our church. I prayed to the Lord, asking for another confirmation: "Lord, if you want me to call this global fast, have this prophet call me out with a word of knowledge using my name and the scripture of Eccles. 11:1, 'Cast your bread upon the waters, for you will find it after many days.'" I asked, "Lord, should I throw out the bread of my revelation of fasting on the waters of history and should we not eat natural food for forty days?" Amazingly, the prophet called me out by my middle name *Dean*, which hardly anyone knew, and said, "You don't know the significance of your name, *Dean*, but a time will come when you'll know." Then he declared, "And I see that you are skinny for you are fasting, and the Lord says, 'Ecclesiastes 11:1, "Cast your bread upon the waters."'"

It was shock and awe! It was as if God had again dropped an atomic bomb in my soul! Needless to say, I began to blow the trumpet and mobilize the fast as far and wide as I could.

Soon after this word, I received an honorary doctorate degree from a Bible school in Los Angeles. When giving me the diploma, the President of the school noticed that the Dean of Students had not signed his name. I immediately knew that this had to do with the prophet's word that it was not yet time to know the significance of my name Dean and its obvious connection with calling the forty-day fast. I think it is interesting to note that Eccles. 11:1 says, "For you will find it after many days." I cast my bread upon the waters, and I don't know how many fasted or how far and wide it spread. But now, as I write this book years later, many nations are hurling themselves into the Jesus Fast. My bread is coming back to me.

After mobilizing fasting for fifteen years through TheCall, suddenly the significance of my name Dean took on new meaning in the person of Dean Briggs.

Detonating the Bomb

Dean Briggs and I had become friends at the International House of Prayer in Kansas City (IHOPKC). One day he asked me a question that shook me to the core and crystallized my life calling. He said, "Lou, if you could preach only one message to ten thousand people, and you knew it would be the catalyst for a global harvest of souls, what would that message be?" Tears flooded my eyes because when God touches you in the core of your calling, you feel it deep in the emotions of your soul. Without hesitation, I replied, "I would call the entire planet to a forty-day fast, because before there was ever an original Jesus Movement, there was an original Jesus Fast." I was stirred to believe that if we would do this, we would see the very results of Jesus' fast and Jesus' evangelistic ministry multiplied worldwide. Dean, a brilliant writer and friend, replied, "Let's write a book! We agreed to call it *The Jesus Fast. The Jesus Fast* is actually a larger volume Dean and I wrote in 2015, filled with prophetic and revelational wisdom concerning the forty-day fast. I encourage you to dig deeper into this subject by reading that original book. Little did I know that once again God was preparing to drop an atomic bomb in my soul as we began to write *The Jesus Fast*.

Shortly after we started writing, an amazing apostolic leader in England, Betty King, put us up in a hotel next to Wembley Stadium in London to continue writing *The Jesus Fast* book. One day we were writing on the atomic bomb of fasting and how fasting inaugurates war in the heavens. We took a break midday and visited the underground bunker where Winston Churchill led England during the Battle of Britain while London was being bombed by the Luftwaffe, the German Air Force. This was when the Royal Air Force miraculously defeated the Luftwaffe and gained air supremacy over England, thus saving the nation. Naturally, our whole day was filled with thoughts about bombs.

Returning to our hotel to finish the chapter, we came face-to-face with a giant obstacle. That obstacle was a yellow restraining ribbon that had been placed in a one-mile radius around Wembley Stadium and our hotel. We approached the policeman standing by the ribbon and said, "We've got to get to our hotel." He replied, "Buddy, you're not getting to your hotel tonight. You're going to have to sleep in a shelter because they've just found an undetonated World War II bomb in the area of your hotel. No one can go beyond this ribbon."

Inwardly, I was a little angry, but I also thought, "This is probably one of those God moments."

So Dean and I decided to walk the circumference of the area and see if we could find a secret lane to sneak into the hotel. As we embarked on this trek, suddenly Dean remembered a dream he had received years ago, one which he described as the most profound spiritual dream of his life. He proceeded to recount it to me.

Amidst talk of war and escalating international conflict, I realize I am an engineer on a top secret mission to deploy and detonate an atomic bomb. As I begin to install it in an open field, a grass fire breaks out, forcing everyone away. I dash to safety and begin to circle on the perimeter, wondering how to get closer so I can finish the task. A friend of mine (who happens to be a life coach) is suddenly present, grabbing fire from the ground and throwing it at me and others. As we run in a circle around the perimeter, he follows me on the inside track, in the flames, repeatedly throwing cinders from the burning ground and saying repeatedly, "Go to the fire, Dean. Go to the fire. Go to the fire!"

I know the bomb has not yet been properly detonated. Finally, I dash forward into the fire, take the bomb, and drive it back into place. As it detonates, an atomic plume mushrooms into the sky. Everything shakes. Certain I will be consumed, I flee, but amazingly I am unharmed.

All of a sudden, the entire sky fills with a message like the largest movie screen in history. Around the planet, nobody can escape the panoramic story of the gospel told straight by God Himself, declaring that what the people of earth have long ignored or mocked is indeed true, but that the window of time to respond is now short. He is coming soon. Judgment cannot be delayed forever. I watch and weep, overwhelmed, for the message in the sky is like Noah's promise. In the dream, a prophetic word had just gone forth from Mike Bickle [founder and director of IHOPKC] that everything was about to change in massive, unpredictable ways, and that we must prepare for it, for the final ingathering of a billion souls was about to launch. Once things shifted, it would become easy to save the lost.

In the dream, I am emotionally overcome and dazed, but I know what I've heard is true. As the vision in the sky fades, I grab the first person to head my way, a twenty-something male. Shell-shocked, he needs no convincing; he just nods, willing and needy for the gospel. I stutter and stumble through a weak, awkward prayer. He mumbles along almost ahead of me, as if the actual prayer were a mere formality because his heart had already made the decision to surrender to Christ. Filled with urgency, I look for the next, and the next. Nearly all are willing. The few that aren't pass by quickly, knowing what I offer. I weep for them, amazed at their stubborn refusal, but there are too many who are willing and too little time to waste. This is the last invitation.

As the dream ends, signs and wonders are breaking out all around. Miracles of healing. Everywhere, waves of anointing to deliver, heal, and save following the simplest preaching of the gospel. It is the most stunning, apocalyptic dream I've ever had; when I wake, I am weeping with God's great love for the lost and a sweet, heavy presence of the Lord fills my bedroom. I quickly glance at my clock.

It is 3:16 a.m.—as in, John 3:16.

As soon as Dean told me his dream, I knew what it meant. In the dream, the atomic bomb represents the atomic power of corporate, extended fasting, as Hall and Bright have written about, and we were writing about that very day. The fire surrounding the bomb was the refining fire of fasting that anyone must go through to gain authority in the Spirit. Mike Bickle, the founder and director of IHOPKC, was symbolic of the end times and massive, united, day-and-night corporate prayer. The billion soul harvest was the masses whose eyes will be opened to the vision of the cross because of fasting, prayer, and evangelism. In summary, this dream was God's unbelievable confirmation to the message we were writing that very day. He was declaring that global prayer and fasting will unleash a spiritual bomb that will break the power of the god of this world who is blinding the eyes of the lost, thus enabling them to see the light of the gospel of the glory of God in the face of Christ. It will unleash a wave of evangelism and missions as has never been seen. John 3:16 will be the great theme of the earth.

This is not theory; it happened following the writing of Hall's book, *Atomic Power With God Thru Fasting and Prayer*, in 1946. Were the revivals of 1948 and the restoration of the nation of Israel that same year a result of massive fasting? Could a global Joel 2 movement of fasting have been fulfilled when after the fast Joel says, "I will restore the land."? and "I will pour out my Spirit on all flesh." Could the evangelistic ministries of Bright, Graham, Osborn and so many others in the same time frame have been part of God's answer to the fasting and prayers of thousands of saints worldwide? Did "The Jesus Fast" (a chapter in Hall's book) cause the mantle of Jesus the Evangelist to fall on so many anointed men and women?

I was absolutely apprehended by the dream and said to Dean, "In the writing of this book, could you, Dean, actually be fulfilling your dream and engineering the detonation of an atomic fasting bomb for global harvest?" It is interesting that next to our hotel was Wembley Stadium. The old English translation of Wembley is "an open field", just like the open field in Dean's dream. And we were circling the hotel where we were writing and detonating that bomb.

Astonishingly, we stumbled upon a lane named Engineer's Lane. Remember, in the dream, Dean was an engineer that detonated bombs. This lane led us to the hotel, and we were allowed to enter. We finished the chapter, and I believe with all my heart that we and many others are detonating the bomb now.

Months later, I was mobilizing for Azusa Now, a massive prayer event, where 70,000 people gathered in the LA Coliseum on the 110th anniversary of the Azusa Street Revival. That day, I was watching my son play soccer and, in the evening, I was scheduled to speak at a certain venue, although I didn't know where that venue was. I didn't want to go back to Pasadena and the Lord sternly forbid me to go to the venue early to prepare. Instead, I booked a hotel just for the afternoon, and there I read the first draft of *The Jesus Fast*. As I was reading, a sudden awareness burst forcefully into my spirit! I realized that Dean Briggs was the answer to Paul Cain's words fifteen years before: "You don't know the significance of your name Dean, but the time will come when you'll know it." That prophecy, remember, was given to me as a confirmation that I was to call a global fast for the harvest. I called Dean Briggs, weeping, and saying, "Dean, remember Paul Cain's prophecy, 'You don't know the significance of your name Dean, but the time will come when you'll know it.' You're the Dean from that prophecy to help me call the world to the forty-day fast!" Our hearts burned together within us on the phone.

Later that evening, my assistant said, "It's time to go to the venue to preach." I had no idea where it was or who it was with, but I simply obeyed my assistant. When we pulled up to the parking lot, I could hardly believe my eyes. The venue was the same building and the same Bible school where I had received my honorary doctorate degree fifteen years before and where the dean's signature had been missing! I could hardly contain myself! The Lord spoke to me, "That was your honorary doctorate degree, but this is your doctoral dissertation. It's time for the global fast for the release of the global harvest. You cast your bread upon the waters and now it is coming back to you."

Hence, this book in your hands could release something of spiritual power akin to Jesus' experience. He came out of the wilderness "in the power of the Spirit" and "the people who sat in darkness saw a great light" (Luke 4:14, Matt. 4:16).

This book is a passion-filled plea for the global Church to commit to extended periods of fasting, even to forty-day fasts, in order to see the greatest harvest of souls the earth has ever seen and usher in the return of the King, Jesus. This is my calling, and I am inviting you to join me in the Jesus Fast!

CHAPTER 2

THE JESUS FAST

There are moments in history when a door for massive change opens. Great revolutions for good or for evil occur in the vacuum created by these openings. It is in these times that key men and women, even entire generations, risk everything to become the hinge of history, that pivotal point that determines which way the door will swing.

The Jesus Fast

Maybe you have heard of The Jesus Movement, that glorious awakening of the 1960s and 1970s, when people were being saved everywhere. Evangelism was so easy! Someone said you could have said "Boo!" and people would get saved. A friend of mine walked up to two guys and asked, "What time is it?" They responded, "It's time for you to get saved." And he did! We have not seen that kind of salvation awakening since that period, and it is the great longing and dream of thousands that we would see another Jesus Movement and way beyond.

There are moments in history when God ushers in the masses to His Kingdom like a combine harvester brings in wheat during the harvest. But while the 60s and 70s were a great era of evangelism, it was not the first or the only Jesus

Movement. As you might guess, the original Jesus Movement started with none other than Jesus Himself.

It is my conviction that the beginning of Jesus' evangelistic ministry, circling around His baptism, His forty-day fast, and His coming out of the wilderness in the power of the Spirit, was not an anomaly, but in some measure, a prototype of every season of harvest in history. They all follow this original pattern.

> When all the people were baptized, it came to pass that Jesus also was baptized; and while He prayed, the heaven was opened. And the Holy Spirit descended in bodily form like a dove upon Him, and a voice came from heaven which said, "You are My beloved Son; in You I am well pleased" . . .Then Jesus, being filled with the Holy Spirit, returned from the Jordan and was led by the Spirit in the wilderness, being tempted for forty days by the devil. And in those days He ate nothing, and afterward, when they had ended, He was hungry . . . Then Jesus returned in the power of the Spirit to Galilee, and news of Him went out through all the surrounding region. And He taught in all their synagogues, being glorified by all.
>
> Luke 3:21-22; 4:1-2,14-15

After His baptism and confirmation of sonship through the Father's voice from heaven, "This is my beloved Son, in whom I am well pleased" (Matt. 3:17), Jesus was immediately driven by the Spirit of God into the wilderness for a prolonged wilderness season of fasting, prayer, and testing. It was during this fast, the Jesus Fast, that He overcame the temptations of Satan and came out in the power of the Holy Spirit with authority over sickness, disease, and demonic oppression.

Many would think that when Jesus was driven by the Spirit into the wilderness to fast for forty days, the weakness of His body during the fast would make Him more susceptible to Satan's temptations. In actuality, the fast strengthened Him in spirit and enabled Him to subdue the power of His flesh so He could overcome. As we said in *The Jesus Fast*, "Adam was tempted with a full stomach in paradise, yet failed. Jesus was tempted in the desert while ravenously hungry, yet succeeded." Jesus was driven by the Spirit into the fast, not just in the weakness of humanity, but as the dread champion Son of God! God was picking a fight with the devil through His own beloved Son. After gaining internal victory over temptation, Jesus went forth in the power of the Spirit with external victory over demons, sickness, disease, and mental illness. It was the Jesus Fast that unleashed the Jesus Movement!

> Fasting begets prophets and strengthens strong men. Fasting makes lawgivers wise; it is the soul's safeguard, the body's trusted comrade, the armor of the champion, the training of the athlete.
>
> Basil, Bishop of Caesarea (AD 330-379)

The Jesus Fast is one of God's weapons for overcoming the enemy of our souls, yes, the world, the flesh, and the devil. It is the fully bent bow that shoots the arrow of the Lord's victory over temptation, thus unleashing the divine destinies of the saints.

Resurgence of Fasting in America

Another wave of united fasting and prayer similar to what began in 1946 broke in the mid-1990s. In 1994, God raised up a leader named Bill Bright to rekindle the flame of fasting in America. An evangelist by calling, Bright founded Campus Crusade for Christ at the University of California, Los Angeles in 1951, and was its president for forty-three years before God burdened him with a call to fasting.

Bright recounted, "In the spring and summer of 1994, I had a growing conviction that God wanted me to fast and pray for forty days for revival in America and for the fulfillment of the Great Commission in obedience to our Lord's command." At first he questioned whether God was truly calling him into this fast. Forty days without food was a daunting task. However, with each passing day, the call of God grew stronger and stronger to fast. Under deep conviction from the Holy Spirit, Bright embarked on his fast with great joy and expectation. He felt that such a long fast was necessary and was God's divine leading because of the magnitude of the sins of America and the Church. He also prayed daily for the acceleration of the fulfillment of the Great Commission. Bright said later that his first forty days of fasting were the most important forty days of his life.

Coming out of his fast, Bright knew he had received a new assignment from the Lord. He said,

> God has never spoken to me audibly, and I am not given to prophecy. But that morning His message to me was clear. "America and much of the world will before the end of the year 2000 experience a great spiritual awakening! And this revival will spark the greatest spiritual harvest in the history of the Church."

I sensed the Holy Spirit was telling me that millions of believers must seek God with all their hearts in fasting and prayer before He will intervene to save America. I was impressed by the Spirit to pray that two million believers will humble themselves by seeking God through forty-day fasts.

In response to this encounter, Bright began to write his book on fasting called *The Coming Revival: America's Call to Fast, Pray, and "Seek God's Face"*. He actually compared fasting with the power of an atomic bomb, echoing Franklin Hall's understanding from 1946. He also gathered six hundred Christian leaders in Orlando in December of 1994 for two days to cry out in prayer and fasting for an awakening in America and for the advancement of the Kingdom of God in the world. I don't believe it is a coincidence that six months later on June 18, 1995, the Brownsville Revival broke out in Pensacola, Florida, which led to tens of thousands being saved and healed over the following years. Who knows how many ministries were birthed as well?

Bright's influence and passion for the renewed subject of fasting were contagious. When his book was released in 1995, it stirred an incredible cross-denominational and international response, sparking hundreds of thousands to fast and pray. In assurance that God was going to release a great spiritual awakening by 2000, Bright called the Church to fast according to God's mandate in 2 Chron. 7:14,

If My people who are called by My name will humble themselves, and pray and seek My face, and turn from their wicked ways, then I will hear from heaven, and will forgive their sin and heal their land.

Bright strongly encouraged every pastor and Christian leader to fast at least one forty-day fast in their lifetime. While Bright was convinced that revival was coming, he believed that the scope of this revival would depend greatly upon how believers responded to the call to fast and pray.[1]

I remember talking to a well-known YWAM leader during this time. This leader told me that he had nearly given up hope for America and resigned himself to reaching other nations with the gospel instead. However, when he heard of Bright's call to fast, he said, "Now I am filled with hope."

When I read Bright's book, faith was born in my heart, and I committed to a forty-day fast in January of 1996. When a great and humble leader like Bright, who created and built one of the largest and most successful college ministries and missions organizations in the world, calls for a fast, that is not the time to argue and debate over religious doctrines or question the merits of the timing of this call to action. It is easy to shrink back from a call like this and fail to make history with God because our flesh doesn't want to fast. As Derek Prince said, fasting is "a tremendous lesson in establishing who the master and who the servant are. Remember, your body is a wonderful servant, but a terrible master." I heard the call, denied my flesh, and began to fast.

This was in 1996, and it was my first forty-day fast. As I wrote earlier, it was during this fast that I heard the intense, audible command of the Lord: "Stretch forth a wakening rod over the earth! Will you do that?" Notice the word said "over the earth!" Since that moment, I have been bound in Spirit to obey this command, and I am stretching that wakening rod in the writing of this book. As you can see, my life's divine purpose of calling the globe to extended seasons of forty-day

---

1   http://www.sermonindex.net/modules/newbb/viewtopic.php?topic_id=58571&forum=35

fasts did not originate with me. I am convinced it came from God and was handed down to me by great fasting fathers of the faith, like Franklin Hall, Derek Prince, and Bill Bright. My hope is that you will join the story. As stated in *The Jesus Fast*, "History may be shaped in the halls of academia and power wielded by fools, financiers, and politicians, but in the halls of heaven, history is shaped by intercessors."

CHAPTER 3

THE *EKBALLO* FAST

The number of missionaries on the field depends entirely on the extent to which someone obeys that command (Matthew 9:38) and prays out the laborers.

Andrew Murray

If added power attends the united prayer of two or three, what mighty triumphs there will be when hundreds of thousands of consistent members of the Church are with one accord, day by day making intercession for the extension of Christ's kingdom.

John R. Mott

Martin Luther wrote one of the greatest hymns in church history, titled "A Mighty Fortress Is Our God". One of the verses declares a mighty truth: "For still our ancient foe doth seek to work us woe; his craft and power are great, and, armed with cruel hate . . . The Prince of Darkness grim, we tremble not for him; his rage we can endure, for lo, his doom is sure, *one little word shall fell him*!"

Can you believe with me that God's Word, even one word, when fully accepted and acted upon, will break Satan's spell over the earth and result in a massive shift in human salvation history? I believe you can. I write this chapter to call the

Church back to one simple, sovereign word found in one revolutionary verse, Matthew 9:38.

> The harvest truly is plentiful, but the laborers are few. *Therefore pray the Lord of the harvest to send out laborers into His harvest.*
> (Matt. 9:37-38, emphasis mine)

No doubt you have heard this before, as have I, but to be honest, I had never really *heard* it.

I don't claim originality or sophistication, just a roaring desire to obey. My convictions are simple:

1. Christ Himself commanded this word.
2. We have generally neglected this word, therefore its potency has never been fully tested.
3. History depends on its fulfillment.

Our neglect was never acceptable, yet it is even less so now. In the fullness of time God *sent* His Son. Another fullness of time of *sending* is upon us. And that *sending* depends entirely on the Church worldwide united in praying this single word and verse of Scripture. In it we have been entrusted with fuel for a global revival. Matthew 9:38 packs enough dynamite to spark a worldwide reformation of evangelism and missions, mobilize tens of thousands of missionaries and reformers, and bring back King Jesus to the planet. In fact, I daresay the absence of a final great harvest is not primarily due to the lack of sincere evangelistic effort or commitment, but principally due to the inconsistency and lack of fervor with which we have attended to this verse, for it is the Lord of the Harvest's most elementary harvest strategy. Heaven's program for evangelization is a prayer idea launched in red type in the Red-Letter Bible.

For me, the revelation and burning desire to pray Matthew 9:38 disrupted my world in late 2011. The YWAM leaders—Andy Byrd, Brian Brennt and their small company—entered my comfortable living room in Kansas City and began to prophesy, "There is coming a shift to TheCall, and it will not be just fasting and prayer but the proclamation of the gospel, signs and wonders, and stadiums will be filled and Billy Graham's mantle is falling on the nation. TheCall will lead to The Send." Heaven rested on our little gathering. I began to ask myself, "Maybe TheCall has been a temporary, John the Baptist-type forerunner to an even greater Jesus Movement, reaping a harvest in America and the nations and leading to a massive sending forth of laborers into the unreached peoples of the earth." As I was pondering this, these YWAM leaders shared their vision for eighty million souls to be saved, resulting in two hundred thousand "sent ones". There would come wave after wave of missionaries breaking into the inner cities, the universities, the closed nations and the unreached people groups with the Good News. But how could so many be saved and sent? We would soon find the prescription for that problem.

On the second day, as we were about to adjourn our meeting, a prophet called my friend and asked if he knew where Lou Engle was. Yes. I was there at that very moment. The prophet told my friend to tell me that he had just received a visitation from the Lord telling me in similar words that there was coming a shift to TheCall and that Billy Graham's mantle was coming on the nation and stadiums would be filled. I knew then that this was the confirmation of the word of the Lord.

There was more to come. Enter that *one little word*!

A year later, while traveling with the same YWAM Circuit Riders, I found myself in Orlando. Once more their prophecies began to stir me. Our sense of the scope of God's purpose in this moment of history was being enlarged even further. Brian Brennt began to rehearse our prophetic storyline, excitedly informing us of a "swirl of God" that had recently transpired in California. He had been with a group of leaders there discussing our history and describing to them the vision of The Send, stadium meetings, and the strategy of gatherings that intentionally joined prayer and evangelism. While admitting that he wasn't quite sure what the name of these gatherings prior to The Send should have, a prophetic leader from Canada, Faytene Grasseschi, suddenly interjected, "The name will be *Ekballo*!" It seemed inspired, but no one was exactly sure what that meant, so they began to research this ancient Greek word.

The answer forms a prayeradigm shift for all of us, and it is the word and reason for the writing of this chapter.

Ancient Word Reborn: Ekballo!

Ekballo is the word Jesus uses in Matthew 9:38, where He instructs His disciples to "pray the Lord of the Harvest to send forth (*ekballo* in Greek) laborers into the harvest field." What is striking is that *ekballo* is not the normal term for "send" as most of our translations have it. A general definition of sending is "to cause to go or be taken, or to arrange for delivery." It is a perfectly useful word for the agreeable transfer of a thing from one place to another. I can send greetings, mail, and money, all with relative ease. *Ekballo*, on the other hand, is neither polite nor restrained. *Ekballo* is far more strident and spiritually confrontational, filled with passion and force. It is used when Paul is "thrown" into prison (Acts 16:37) and Stephen is "cast out" of the city and stoned (Acts 7:58). You see, *ekballo* is not pretty. It is effective, but it is not pretty. If we applied Greek to baseball, we would understand that pitchers don't send the ball out of their hand toward the batter at home plate, they *ekballo* the ball! This is the same word Jesus uses when he says, "If I by the finger of God, cast out (*ekballo*) demons, then the Kingdom of Heaven has come upon you" (Luke 11:20). Whoa! You realize, demons do not come out willingly, right? They must be *ekballo'd*! Great force must overcome great resistance.

When Jesus *ekballos* demons, demons gotta go! When Jesus *ekballos* laborers, evangelists and missionaries gotta go! Thus, *ekballo* is a verb of intense spiritual energy and force. *Ekballo* vehemence is necessary to disrupt the convenient lives of recalcitrant, under-envisioned laborers. Everything about extended fasting and world missions threatens our comfort. We greatly love our comfortable homes and insularity. That's why Jesus commands His disciples to implore the Lord of the Harvest to *ekballo* laborers. Something strong and forceful must grip us. In Mark 12 we read that the Spirit drove (*ekballo'd*) Jesus into the wilderness to fast. Jesus was gripped with an intense desire to enter the fast. Anytime one gets an intense desire to fast, you can bet it isn't the devil tempting them. No! Something is getting ready to break!

Dick Simmons: The Cross and the Switchblade

Dick Simmons had no idea of the divine energy he was releasing that midnight hour as he prayed *ekballo* from Matthew 9:38. Overlooking the Hudson River and burdened for the New York City gangs, he begged with loud cries to the Lord of the Harvest to thrust forth workers into that harvest field. The police came to arrest him for disturbing the peace. When the police found him praying, they refused to disturb the praying man. On the very night he was praying, it was later discovered, a young man in Pennsylvania saw an article and photograph in the 1958 edition of *Life Magazine* of seven teenagers who were members of a gang in New York City. The Holy Spirit moved him so powerfully with compassion that he was stirred to go to New York City to preach to them.

History records the young man's name as David Wilkerson. *The Cross and the Switchblade* book, the conversion of Nicky Cruz, Teen Challenge, thousands of drug addicts and gang members converted, Times Square Church, millions impacted by the gospel through the life and ministry of David Wilkerson —all this because one man cried *ekballo* into the quiet night. David Wilkerson recently joined the great cloud of witnesses and all the world knows his name, but who knows Dick Simmons? I tell you, heaven knows Dick Simmons! One man praying one verse, Matthew 9:38, thrust forth one laborer. And behold the harvest! Tens of thousands of souls will not only be credited to Wilkerson's account, but also to the account of a praying man. Ever has it been that history goes to the intercessor. The person who went and the person who prayed both reap the harvest and both receive their eternal reward.

The question must be asked: Would David Wilkerson have been thrust forth into the harvest if Dick Simmons had not prayed Matthew 9:38?

I received the answer to my own question in the most profound way soon after my Orlando *ekballo* whirlwind. It is the reason I am under divine constraint to call the Church to pray this verse faithfully. While reading the classic book *Rees Howells: Intercessor*, I was suddenly arrested by the following paragraph:

> For years Mr. Howells had been praying for the gospel to go to the world. Before he went to Africa, the Spirit brought before him God's promise to His Son in Psalm 2:8. He had not let a day pass without praying that the Savior should have "the heathen for His inheritance and the uttermost parts of the earth for His possession," and it was in willingness to be, in some measure, the answer to his own prayers that he had accepted the call to Africa. Then, while in Africa, he had been struck by Andrew Murray's comment on the Savior's words in Matthew 9:38, "Pray ye therefore the Lord of the harvest that He will send forth laborers into His harvest." *Andrew Murray has pointed out, on the strength of this verse, that the number of missionaries on the field depends entirely on the extent to which someone obeys that command and prays out the laborers*; and the Lord had called Mr. Howells to do this.

As I read this, I could not describe the effect of these words on my soul. It was as if every other vision fled from the intensity of their light. In one moment I knew my whole life would be completely consumed with this call. There in that book right beside, "And the Lord had called Mr. Howells to do this," I wrote, "And the Lord has called Lou Engle to do this."

A vision came to me of raising up a million believers worldwide who would pray Matthew 9:38 daily. Pray! *Ekballo!*

Read this one statement by Andrew Murray again and let it grip you as it gripped me. "The number of missionaries on the field depends entirely on the extent to which someone obeys that command and prays out the laborers."

Depends. *Entirely.* Depends entirely! *Entirely!*

If Andrew Murray, one of the great revivalists and missionary statesmen in church history, and one of the greatest Bible teachers and authors in this past century, makes this outrageous claim as I believe the scripture does, should we not weigh it and be shaken by its implications?

If this scripture and Andrew Murray's commentary is true and the Church really grasped its importance, then overnight, Matthew 9:38 would become the fiery petition of millions of lips across the planet. Every single day we would not relent. Sadly, it is not so. Why? Consider the massive challenges we face: millions in America without Christ; our inner cities ravaged with hopelessness, violence, and destruction; over seven thousand unreached people groups on earth today with 3.2 billion people having never heard the gospel. Yet if Andrew Murray was right, the great overwhelming problem of the harvest is not primarily our lack of laborers, *for the Lord of the Harvest has promised to ekballo them*! It is primarily our disobedience to His command to pray this prayer. I am shaken by this.

> *Have I taken Matthew 9:38 merely as a suggestion?*
> *Have I trivialized the prayer that finishes the mission?*

I believe an earth-shaking revolution is about to take place because the Lord of the Harvest is once again breathing upon the prayer He told us to pray. If the first apostles were commanded to pray this prayer before they were sent and as they were going, how much more will the last apostolic generation be required by heaven to pray this prayer? Friends, we are nearing the end of the story. The final horizon is coming into view and the stage is being set for the return of Christ. "The harvest is the end of the age" (Matt. 13:39), yet still Jesus cries out, "The harvest is plentiful but the laborers are few. Pray the Lord of the Harvest to *ekballo* laborers into His harvest fields."

Understanding Ekballo: "I Command You to Beg Me."

This *ekballo* moment in Matthew 9 is a climactic moment in Jesus' ministry. Jesus is going to reveal the remedy to the great problem which is not the plentiful harvest but the lack of workers to reap it. The King James Version adds a vital emphasis. In light of this problem, "pray ye therefore!"

Pray the Lord of the harvest to send out laborers into His harvest!

If we skim along Matthew 9:38 too quickly, it may seem we are listening to a casual exchange between Jesus and His disciples rather than hearing the marching orders of the Lord of the Harvest. If you are like me, in the past you might have read the verse as a simple exhortation to pray from time to time for laborers to get a greater burden for souls. However, when we examine it in context, the language convinces us otherwise.

In the preceding verses Jesus is healing the sick, preaching the gospel of the Kingdom, and driving out demons. When He sees the massive crowds coming to Him harassed and helpless, like sheep without a shepherd, He is broken to pieces with compassion. Overwhelmed by the limitations of His own incarnation, He is gripped with the need of thousands who can minister like Himself. Immediately, He gathers His disciples and, filled with an explosive passion, forcefully exhorts them to pray. No! Not just pray! *Deēthēte*, the Greek word for "pray" used here is not the common word used for prayer in the New Testament; rather, it means to beseech and beg earnestly, to entreat with urgent intensity. It is not a passive, under-your-breath type of prayer, but a resounding cry of intensity and passion. Jesus is not calling His disciples to a bloodless, passionless and vague prayer. He is commanding them to shake heaven with their voices until laborers are hurled forth!

As we examine the Greek word further, we see that it is used in what is called the aorist imperative verb tense. To His original listeners, the Lord's exhortation would have sounded more like this, "I command you to beg Me and keep on begging Me!" These words, taken as the original Greek intended them to be understood, could bring a revolution to the worldwide prayer movement. Jesus is not giving His disciples a polite suggestion. He is not asking them to fit this prayer into their schedule every now and then. No! He is unbridling His own intensity so that they feel constrained by the burden of it.

Brothers and sisters, if there was any other alternative that could better remedy the radical world evangelism problem of too few laborers, don't you think Jesus would have inserted that solution in Matthew 9 instead? If prayer was merely one of many good ideas, why wouldn't He have simply said to go? Why risk praying if it wastes our already limited time? I feel a little like a broken record, but the Lord of the Harvest Himself is commanding the primary method of harvest, and it is one, single, active, passionate, imperative verb: Beg!

I mentioned earlier that for some time I didn't know what my role was in the coming together of the missions and prayer movements. But I have found my answer! *Ekballo* is where the prayer movement and missions movements collide. The prayers of *ekballo* are what fuel the missions movement, and I am committed to pray and mobilize the *ekballo* prayer until every nation is reached and Jesus returns.

In 2013, responding to the *ekballo* prophecy, we launched the Ekballo House of Prayer in Pasadena, California. Once again the little word *ekballo* exploded off the pages of Scriptures. While reading Mark 2:1, we saw that Jesus was driven by the Spirit into the wilderness. The word "driven" in the Greek is also *ekballo*. Fasting intensifies prayer, so we began the House of Prayer with a forty-day fast from March 1 through April 9, begging "*Ekballo*!" For seven years we have entered into this forty-day Jesus Fast, or *Ekballo* Fast, praying Matthew 9:38. God has responded to the prophecies and these fasts powerfully. In February 2019, the shift took place. TheCall became The Send. On February 20, at Camping World Stadium in Orlando, 60,000 people gathered to be sent out into the harvest fields of the earth. Three stadiums will be filled in Brazil on February 8, 2020, for The Send. And it is spreading. People are dreaming dreams and receiving callings. "Who shall go for me and whom shall I send?" God is responding to those forty-day *ekballo* fasts. What if the whole Church, as in Bill Bright's days, would unite in fasting for forty days and crying "*Ekballo!*" with one voice? I see waves of evangelists and missionaries hurled forth, sweeping across the globe with the proclamation of the gospel. Jesus' command will be answered. It shall be fulfilled!

CHAPTER 4

THE FAST THAT UNLOCKS SALVATION

One thing I know: that though I was blind, now I see.
John 9:25

In 1984, my Pastor Che Ahn and a team of twelve of us planted a church in Pasadena, California. God led us in a strategy of intercession that connects the power of fasting and the release of power for salvation. We saw how through fasting and worship the veil that covers and blinds the eyes of the lost can be removed so they can be saved. At one point we had come under a burden to pray that a prophetic anointing would come so powerfully in our corporate worship services that people would be saved just being in the presence of the Lord. We prayed that it would be like David when he played his harp and drove away a tormenting spirit from Saul. Why couldn't we see the same thing?

So about ten to fifteen of us fasted and prayed for thirty days and held evening meetings every night. We focused our prayers like laser beams on one thing: "Lord, loose the power of Your presence in worship with such power that people will get saved without an altar call!"

There is something to be said about extended fasting and prayer for breakthrough. Many times we fast but we are not really clear what the objective of our intercession is. There are other times in our prayer life when we go for a breakthrough, focusing on one thing, and will not take no for an answer! We are conclusive. We have set our face!

On the twenty-ninth night of that fast, I was reading the passage where Saul came among the sons of the prophets who were prophesying and playing their instruments. An anointing came over the king of the nation of Israel, and he fell down and prophesied, all day long. We've got a little way to go before we touch the dimension of worship that causes kings to prophesy for twenty-four hours! To get there, we can't just be satisfied with good worship albums. When I read that, I began to experience a genuine travail of the Holy Spirit. I began to groan in the spirit, knowing the following day was the thirtieth day of fasting, coinciding with our Sunday morning worship. We weren't a weird church, we weren't dancing crazies or fanatics, but that morning the guitar player began to play spontaneous chords and I began to sing a new song: "We gaze upon Your purity, we gaze upon Your purity, we gaze upon Your loveliness, holy incense do we bring, and we gaze into an open heaven." When I sang that line, heaven opened. It was like a bomb dropped in the congregation. A holy pandemonium broke out, people were dancing, shouting, and screaming, "We see angels!" some shouted. Heaven invaded the place. No one could preach. God Himself was preaching. People began to get saved right during worship. And for weeks, during worship, we would give the opportunity for people to respond and they would get saved. We experienced a major breakthrough for evangelism through worship, as it sprung from the boiler room of fasting and prayer. We saw in graphic demonstration the connection between the breakthrough into salvation and the removing of the veil through fasting and prayer that precedes the breakthrough. Remember Dean's dream at the beginning of this book? It was the nuclear explosion of fasting and prayer that cleared

THE FAST THAT UNLOCKS SALVATION

the skies of the powers of darkness in the second heaven that led to the billion soul harvest. Our little breakthrough was a microcosm of the harvest that will come when the Church will unite in one accord in global fasting.

The Sons of Thunder

> Then a herald cried aloud: "To you it is commanded, O peoples, nations, and languages, that at the time you hear the sound of the horn, flute, harp, lyre, and psaltery, in symphony with all kinds of music, you shall fall down and worship the gold image that King Nebuchadnezzar has set up (Dan. 3:4-5)

> I don't care who writes your laws. If I can write your music I can shape your destiny. (Unknown)

In 2009, I was going into a forty-day fast in Kansas City. Before I entered into the fast, I dreamed that my belly was undergoing an operation. I woke praying, "God, are you trying to operate on my appetite so that I can be a Daniel that shifts history through prayer and fasting?"

In the middle of that fast, a prophetic intercessor emailed me with a dream. In the dream I was lying down sleeping and I was fasting. Five angels came into my bedroom and operated on my belly. Then they took the Book of Daniel, lit it on fire, and sealed it into my belly. The scene changed and all these young people were coming to me wearing t-shirts that said, "Sons of Thunder." For ten years now I have believed that, like Daniel, who, when he understood that it was time for the Jewish jailbreak out of Babylon, fasted and prayed to initiate that mass exodus, the Church would be led by God in a *kairos* time to enter into forty-day fasts that would release the new breed of musicians, Sons of Thunder. Could we be in that fast now?

Music is the most powerful force to shape the destiny of generations. When you consider the mass hysteria and sudden worldwide hypnosis created by The Beatles, you realize how at the right time and place a sound could frame the future of the globe. In the early 1960s, the world was under the spell of a great expectation for a new world order and a new song of freedom. It was the dawning of the Age of Aquarius. The Beatles seized that moment and created a sound that helped frame the counterculture of the 60s. Like in the days of Daniel, The Beatles music captured a sound that called the masses to fall down and worship. Now, in this pregnant moment in history, where are the prophet musicians who will fast and pray and pay the price to pull down from heaven the sound of the Great Singer of Songs that will call masses to fall down and worship, this time the only One worthy of worship?

Years ago a prophet named James Ryle saw three dreams. The dreams concerned a new music and a new breed of evangelistic musicians to come. These musicians were called Sons of Thunder. The first dream portrayed a traveling evangelistic truck whose side would roll down to create a stage for a band to play in the streets. Behind the curtain in that truck were a couple of young men playing their blue guitars. They weren't playing for a stage or a label. They were playing to an audience of One. Their music had a prophetic (blue) sound born out of deep intimacy with God. They had in their hands sheet music for a new song that would arrest the world with its sound, similar to how The Beatles captured the world with their sound and shaped the unrighteous counterculture of the 1960s and 1970s. The only difference was that this new song was of God and was meant for righteous purposes.

In the second dream, Ryle was taken to a large church which had a stage. Off in the corner of a storage closet was a power amplifier. The amp was unplugged and dusty, like it had been sitting in the corner for a while. Then, what he saw took his breath away! He gasped with a sense of discovery when he realized that what he held in his hand was the power amp that The Beatles had used!

Suddenly, he was out of the equipment room and standing behind the pulpit at a church, still holding the amp. The church had grown to five times the size that it was at the beginning of the dream. A woman stood up in the middle of the church and a light shone on her. She began singing a song of the Lord and all she sang was, "In the name of Jesus Christ the Lord we say unto you, be saved!" She sang it over and over. She would turn to her right and sing, then turn to her left and sing; then she would turn behind her and front of her and sing the same words. As Ryle watched her sing, men and women were collapsing in their seats, converted to Christ, just by the power of that song.

When he woke up, the Lord said that there was coming an anointing and sound out of the Church that would have a spiritual power greater than that of The Beatles, and people would simply be saved under the anointing of these new songs. Sons of Thunder—evangelists, worshipers, and evangelist-worshipers—would come to release this sound.

For years this dream has been hanging in the intercessory consciousness of God's praying people. "For the vision is yet for an appointed time; but at the end it will speak, and it will not lie. Though it tarries, wait for it; because it will surely come, it will not tarry" (Hab. 2:3). Many times God's dreams and visions tarry long but when they finally come to pass they do not delay. They come with sudden outrageous drama. Media blows up, heads spin, it becomes the current conversation of the masses. Isn't that what happened with The Beatles? One moment on the Ed Sullivan Show and The Beatles sound bomb went off and stadiums were filled with adoring throngs! I hear the coming of another sudden sound bomb, an atomic explosion fueled by fasting and prayer with musicians paying the price no other generation has been willing to pay in order to hear and release the songs heaven is singing. Millions will be saved and healed! Stadiums will be filled! Here come Sons of Thunder! The *Ekballo* Fast has moved heaven and the Great God has hurled the musicians forth into the arena where angels reap and devils rage. At the time of writing, Kanye West has confessed his conversion to Christ, and thousands are gathering and many are being saved at his outdoor Sunday worship services. It is taking the nation by storm. It is coming with sudden outrageous drama. Maybe he is one of the Sons of Thunder. It is like The Beatles. Pray for this man to be kept by the power of God.

CHAPTER 5

THE BRIDAL LOVE FAST

Oh, I have slipped the surly bonds of earth, and danced the skies on laughter-silvered wings; Sunward I've climbed and joined the tumbling mirth of sun-split clouds—and done a hundred things You have not dreamed of— wheeled and soared and swung high in the sunlit silence. Hovering there I've chased the shouting wind along and flung my eager craft through footless halls of air. Up, up the long delirious burning blue I've topped the wind-swept heights with easy grace, where never lark, or even eagle, flew; and, while with silent, lifting mind I've trod the high untrespassed sanctity of space, put out my hand and touched the face of God.

"High Flight", a poem by John Gillespie Magee, Jr

John Gillespie Magee Jr. was a fighter pilot in World War II. He penned this amazing poem on the freedom of flight. He died in an air crash at the age of 19, but not before leaving the world this poetry of shimmering imagery comparing the natural ecstasy of flight, its soaring to unknown heights and its feeling of unfettered freedom to the extreme pleasures of actually reaching up and touching the face of God.

The definition of surly: ill-tempered, glum, morose, moody, uncivil, sour, grumpy.

How rough and crusty and how ill-tempered this earthbound existence seems when compared to the ecstasy of touching God! In 1906, prior to the great Azusa Street Revival, Frank Bartleman had a face-to-face encounter with Jesus. He said that for days afterward he could hardly hold a human conversation because of its unseemly earthly surliness. John Wesley, when he visited the early Moravian community and experienced firsthand its first love encounter with the abiding Presence, commented, "I dwelt among a people whose conversation was in heaven."

> Largely through the grace of fasting, I have come to deeply know the liberating flight of freedom, from the common and profane, to the call of the wild. Fasting has given me wings. (*The Jesus Fast*)

The prophet Joel admonishes the nation to return to God with all their heart, with fasting, weeping, and mourning (Joel 2:12). Fasting is a God-given means to return to first love encounter with Jesus. Fasting softens the soul, that impertinent part of your being that demands the feeding of the flesh, that surly part that wants its own way that demands to be fed. The fleshly soul is a hard taskmaster. In fasting we command that soul to obey the spirit. In fasting, the food lusts, sexual desires, and greed grasps are diminished and the spiritual desires inside us become strong. The spirit man who has been crying within us so long, "Feed me!" is strengthened with power and is drawn to God.

The first time I fasted, it seemed that heaven came so close to me. In almost every fast I have ever undertaken, within a few days my soul has opened to the tenderness and the presence of Jesus, tears have begun to flow, and my heart has found its first love home again.

Jesus, when asked by John's disciples, "Why do your servants not fast?" said, "The days will come when the bridegroom will be taken away from them, and then they will fast" (Matt. 9:15). This was not a rebuke to John's disciples. Jesus was saying, "You are living in a three-year dispensation, a new wineskin, when I, the Bridegroom, am with you. But when I go and the Holy Spirit comes, I will inaugurate a new era of fasting that will take John's fasting to an even higher level and intensity!" The Church, as the Bride of Christ, will long for Him and His coming in an even greater measure than John, just as the bride loves the bridegroom even more than the friend of the bridegroom. The Bride's fasting will be the channel for her ever-increasing longings for His presence and return. Fasting is the God-given flight pattern into the ecstasy of love.

God, through the prophet Jeremiah, declared over the children of Israel, "I remember the devotion of your youth, your love as a bride, how you followed Me in the wilderness" (Jer. 2:2 BSB)! It is in the wilderness of the forty-day fast that we find the flight of freedom from the surly bonds of earth. All of these lesser pleasures usurping our soul's affections are stripped away, and we, being dead to everything, experience resurrection power and find pleasures at His right hand.

The angel for the church of Ephesus wounds and warns the saints there with these burning words, "Nevertheless I have this against you, that you have left your first love" (Rev. 2:4). In fasting you don't just lose weight, you break the gravitational pull of earthly things and set your mind on things above. You return to your first love. And sometimes during or after the fast you slip the surly bonds of earth, dance the skies, tread the untrespassed sanctity of space, and touch the face of God. My friend Bill Johnson writes in his challenging book, *Face to Face with God*, "The quest for the face of God is the ultimate quest. But to embrace the quest for the face of God, one must be ready to die." This is why I am calling the Body of Christ to extended seasons of fasting, to die to everything, to return to the devotion of her youth, to once again follow her Bridegroom into the wilderness, to long for a face-to-face encounter, His coming now in a worldwide revival and His second coming when we will rule with Him on the earth, when we shall behold His glory.

Show Me Your Glory

Moses said, "Please show me your glory." . . . And He said, "I will make all my goodness pass before you and will proclaim before you my name 'The Lord.'" (Ex. 33:18 ESV)

Fasting is not a tool for gaining discipline or piety. Instead, fasting is the . . . act of ridding ourselves of fullness to attune our senses to the mysteries that swirl in and around us. Sometimes God shows up. Sometimes he feeds us. And every now and then, He throws His wild glory before us like bursting constellations. (Dan Allender)

Our days of corporate fasting were high days indeed. Never have we been closer to the Central Glory! (Charles H. Spurgeon)

I have never had a face-to-face encounter with Jesus; I have never seen His Shekinah Glory. I have had two glorious dreams in which I heard the unbelievable music of the angelic choir and saw the majestic waterfall of God. But it has been primarily through my fasting that God has taken the dimness of my soul away and heavenly things have become more real. I remember the first fast I ever did. At the time, my job was mowing lawns in Maryland. On the third day, the presence of the Lord swirled around me. I felt as if I could touch the angels. It was a rare ecstasy, and from that point I have been ruined for the pleasures of fasting. Gravity lost its pull on me and I made my home in rarified air. In ridding my soul of fullness, I was being attuned to the mysteries that swirled around me. The realm of dreams was opened and I could hear the whisper of God more clearly. In those dreams I had a glimpse of eternity. At times in fasting, the veil of the soul becomes very thin, and it is almost like you can reach out your hand through that thin veneer and behold the glory of God like Moses did on his forty-day fast. What if thousands around the globe subdued the lesser pleasures of their flesh through extended fasting and cried out like Moses, "Show me your glory!"?

Bread from Heaven

> But he answered, "It is written, 'Man shall not live by bread alone, but by every word that comes from the mouth of God.'" (Matt. 4:4 ESV)

In this passage, Jesus quotes from the book of Deuteronomy where Israel wandered in the wilderness for forty years. God sought to train His people that manna from heaven is far more satisfying than the sweet bread of earth. What a generation failed in over the course of forty years, Jesus fulfilled through a forty-day fast. A forty-day fast can feed you with bread from heaven, shorten the span of testing in your life, and break the cycle of temptation and failure. Oh! You want bread from heaven!

I will never forget driving with seven men in the lawn maintenance truck. While they were high, smoking marijuana, I was feasting on the revelation of who I was in Christ in the Book of Ephesians. I found that Jesus is truly the Living Bread. During this fast, I'd encourage you to pray for a spirit of wisdom and revelation in the knowledge of God (Eph. 1:17). Instead of cooking and eating, you now have all that time to read and ingest the Word of God. Fasting is not only abstaining from food, it is feasting on God and His Word!

CHAPTER 6

THE FAST TO PRECIPITATE THE LATTER RAIN

We feel the rains of your love
We feel the winds of your spirit
Now the heartbeat of heaven
Let us hear

Let it rain, let it rain
Open the floodgates of heaven
Let it rain

Pocket Full of Rocks

The accumulated voices of 400,000 young people swelled, as the band Pocket Full of Rocks led them in singing the anthem "Let It Rain". I could hardly contain myself. That day I had asked the band to lead the great throng with that song alone. They had written "Let It Rain" several years before, and I was privileged to lead the Rock the Nations intercessory prayer gatherings under the anointing of that powerful song. The song was hidden in the desert, so to speak, until the day of its public appearance. On September 2, 2000, at TheCall DC, Michael W. Smith heard the song and was deeply moved by it, recorded it on his album, and it exploded worldwide. The song has never lost its anointing. Why? Because God wants the Church worldwide to cry for the latter rain.

During a protracted forty-day fast in 1996, I saw an epic dream. In the dream, I was with two leaders of a ministry that I worked with called Rock the Nations. There was a young boy with these leaders whose name was Joel. In the dream, I was supposed to be giving Joel a letter, but I had lost it and was frantically looking for it. I woke out of the dream, and immediately the Lord spoke to my heart, "Don't lose Joel's letter. Call the youth of America to fasting and prayer." In response to that dream, we mobilized 400,000 youth to the National Mall in Washington, D.C. to fast and pray for America. Joel's letter, the Book of Joel in the Bible, is a blueprint preparation for the outpouring of the Spirit.

In the Book of Joel, the prophet speaks of a day when the Spirit of God would be poured out on all people worldwide. That outpouring would be preceded by a mass movement of fasting and repentance.

> Consecrate a fast, call a sacred assembly; gather the elders and all the inhabitants of the land into the house of the Lord your God, and cry out to the Lord . . . And it shall come to pass afterward that I will pour out My Spirit on all flesh. (Joel 1:14, 2:28)

Peter quoted this same passage on the day of Pentecost.

> But this is what was spoken by the prophet Joel: "And it shall come to pass in the last days, says God, that I will pour out My Spirit on all flesh; your sons and your daughters shall prophesy, your young men shall see visions, your old men shall dream dreams." (Acts 2:16-17)

Notice the subtle, yet extremely important difference between these two passages of scripture. Joel states that "It shall come to pass afterward," whereas Peter states that, "It shall come to pass in the last days." From the context of Joel, we understand that the word afterward means 'after the Fast'. Joel's fast would precipitate the outpouring of the Holy Spirit. Peter changes the word "afterward" into "the last days". Putting it together we understand two things. First, widespread fasting and prayer leads to outpourings of the Holy Spirit. Secondly, there will be a global fasting movement, which will lead to a global outpouring of the Spirit in the last days.

Turning back to Joel 2, we find that Joel gave us a blueprint and time frame for when and how God will pour out His Spirit in the last days.

> He has given you the former rain faithfully, and he will cause the rain to come down for you—the former rain, and the latter rain in the first month. (Joel 2:23)

In the natural, the rain in Israel would fall in two seasons to water the land to bring forth the harvest. The seasons were named the *former* and the *latter* rain. Here Joel compares the spiritual outpourings in the last days to the two natural rainy seasons in Israel. The former rain fell on the Early Church at Pentecost and the latter rain is falling on us in these last days of history. God's marker for the beginning and end of the last days is the outpouring of His Spirit. We are living in the days of the latter rain when God has promised to pour out His Spirit like a deluge on the earth.

The first chapter of Joel depicts a scene of spiritual apostasy leading to total economic collapse, agricultural devastation, and judgment of the Lord. Israel has left their God. This isn't too different from America and many nations in the West today. Fortunately, Joel gives a prescription for the return to God. This prescription is united fasting and prayer.

> "Now, therefore," says the Lord, "Turn to Me with all your heart, with fasting, with weeping, and with mourning." (Joel 2:12)

Three times the call to fasting is given. The third and final call is what is known in Hebrew culture as a *chazakah*[1]. When

---

1   http://www.jewishtreats.org/2018/05/three-times-strong.html

a matter is repeated three times, it becomes a precedent, or permanent. By repeating Himself a third time, the Lord is setting a precedent for how His people are supposed to seek Him when the nation has turned from Him. From Joel's time until ours, this precedent is permanent and unchangeable. The precedent is not just prayer; it is repentance, prayer, and fasting! This is what precipitates the latter rain.

Two Books

Years ago a wonder-filled window of revelation and motivation for fasting opened and confirmed my life's job description: calling the globe to a united forty-day fast. I woke one morning with a deep desire, almost an inward groaning, to read two books that had greatly influenced my faith. The first book called *Rain from Heaven* was written by Arthur Wallis, one of the fathers of the charismatic movement in Great Britain. He spoke of the latter rain mentioned in the book of Joel as a picture of the last days outpouring of the Holy Spirit in revival. The other book, *Shaping History Through Prayer and Fasting*, was given to me thirty-five years ago and has been the textbook of my life. It was written by Derek Prince, a great statesman and teacher in the Body of Christ. One of the chapters in Prince's book was titled "Fasting Precipitates the Latter Rain".

Groaning in my spirit that morning, I longed that God would speak to me once again that my calling to mobilize global fasting would help precipitate the latter rain. I needed confirmation to encourage my faith.

I looked in all my bookshelves and could not find either book. The desire in my spirit to read those books was so strong that I found myself groaning all day long, "Lord, help me find these two books today! I need you to confirm to me that fasting precipitates the latter rain." It seemed so strange but it was as if the Holy Spirit had set the stage for this confirmation. He was groaning inside me: "I must help Lou find those books!"

That night I was in Lancaster, California, preparing to preach at my friend Joe Sweet's church. I was sitting in his office preparing and he sat at his desk. Suddenly he rose from his desk, walked over to his bookshelf, and said, "Come here Lou." As I drew near, he reached out and pulled a book off of his shelf and said, "Lou, you're looking for this book." It was *Rain From Heaven*! I could hardly believe my eyes! But I knew that God was roaring over my calling.

The following morning I was teaching a prophetic class, and right before the meeting one of the students walked up to me and said, "Lou, I was at the Anaheim Vineyard Church this morning, and a man shouted to me, 'You're going to see Lou Engle today! Give him this book. He's looking for it!'" The student handed me the book. It was *Shaping History Through Prayer and Fasting*!

That window of encounter in the finding of these books has produced in me one of the most dynamic inward motivations, in season and out of season, to continue in this calling. I am gripped to respond like Elijah did to the promise of the Lord for a coming rain.

> The word of the Lord came to Elijah, in the third year, saying, "Go, present yourself to Ahab, and I will send rain on the earth." . . . Then Elijah said to Ahab, "Go up, eat and drink; for there is the sound of abundance of rain." So Ahab prepared a feast but Elijah climbed to the top of Carmel and fell to the ground and prayed. (1 Kings 18:1, 41 BSB, NLT)

While Ahab went up to eat and drink, Elijah went up to the top of Mount Carmel to fast and pray. He knelt down, put his head between his knees and prayed seven times. Elijah knew by revelation it was time for the rain. Zech. 10:1 commands, "Pray for the rain in the time of the latter rain." After the seventh time of prayer, Elijah's servant declared, "I see a little cloud about the size of a man's hand rising from the sea" (1 Kings 18:44 NLT). Elijah's response to a promise of rain wasn't to sit idly by until it came, but to pray to God until the rain came! A response of faith to a promise of God is to take action through intercession until God has fulfilled His promise! Like Elijah, I too hear the sound of the coming latter rain and have set myself to fast and pray until it comes, for fasting precipitates the latter rain!

In 40 Days I Will Send the Rain

Again, another life-defining dream came to me. In the dream I saw railroad tracks going to the ocean and on those tracks mighty cannons of war were rolling. The tracks entered into a densely wooded jungle and there in the jungle an old man in an old cart, wrapped and entwined in thick vines, brought the cannons to a halt and stopped them from moving forward. While the train sat hopelessly obstructed, suddenly violent warriors appeared and expelled the old man and the old cart with unbelievable intensity. The cannons began to roll again. The scene changed in the dream and a scroll rolled down before me that said, "In yet forty days I will send the rain."

I knew the interpretation of the dream. The cannons rolling to the ocean were the supernatural power of God that was being sent to the nations of the earth. But the old man and the old cart were a spirit of religion that had "the appearance of godliness, but denied its power" (2 Tim. 3:5 ESV). It was a symbol of the dull and uninspired, powerless Church, filled with unbelief. In contrast, the violent warriors represented the spiritual violence of the forty-day fast that could break through religion, expel unbelief, and loose the power of God to the nations. Once again I saw my scroll and the scroll of the Church, promising that following the forty-day fast there would come the release of the latter rain at the end of the age.

Even as I write this chapter, I pray that you might understand why I am compelled to call this global forty-day fast; and in hearing these stories you might find yourself being *ekballo'd* into the wilderness of fasting like Jesus to unleash Christ within you, who is the very power of the age to come.

CHAPTER 7

THE FAST THAT INAUGURATES WAR IN THE HEAVENS

We are so utterly ordinary, so commonplace, while we profess to know a power the twentieth century does not reckon with. But we are "harmless," and therefore unharmed. We are spiritual pacifists, non-militants, conscientious objectors in this battle-to-the-death with principalities and powers in high places . . . We are "sideliners"—coaching and criticizing the real wrestlers while content to sit by and leave the enemies of God unchallenged. The world cannot hate us; we are too much like its own. Oh that God would make us dangerous!

Jim Elliott

A Roman War Goddess

During a forty-day fast in 1996, my friend dreamed of a Buddhist house of prayer on top of a Christian house of prayer, dominating it in a wrestling match. Suddenly, the Christian house of prayer did a reversal and began dominating the Buddhist house of prayer. The Lord spoke to us, "Raise up a house that contends with every other house that exalts itself against the knowledge and supremacy of Christ."

In 1999, I became strikingly aware of a spiritual battleground through a dream that was given to a Peruvian woman of God.

Her dream unveiled the nature of a cosmic spiritual battle and a divine prayer assignment to contend for California. In the dream, she saw a Roman war goddess in a large body of water, heaping up huge waves. People were swimming in those waves but couldn't reach their destinies because of the magnitude of the surging swells.

In the dream, an angel appeared to her and said, "The only thing that can break the power of this spirit is forty days of fasting like Jesus on water." She asked if the dream meant anything to me. Having been an intercessor for California for twenty years, I understood the significance of the revelation. There is a Roman war goddess on the state seal of California, and it sits on San Francisco Bay. Her name is Minerva. In the Roman mythology, Minerva was the goddess of war who made war against men. She was also the goddess of wisdom, arts, and education. If the dream was true, the Lord was revealing that a spiritual entity of darkness seated in San Francisco was controlling California and keeping it from fulfilling its destiny. However, if the dream was true, that spiritual power could be broken with a united forty-day water fast!

Three years went by. I was flying home from TheCall in Seoul, Korea, to mobilize for TheCall San Francisco. As I was flying, the Holy Spirit suddenly reawakened me to the dream of the Peruvian woman and an intense desire welled up within me to do a forty-day water fast to break the power of that spirit over San Francisco. Along with that deep stirring, a deep fear also came upon me. I had never done a forty-day fast on water alone, and I began to wonder if I would die. I wrestled with God for some time and prayed, "God, I don't want to die, but I want to do this fast." The Lord spoke very strongly to me. "Do you love California enough to die for it?" I answered, "Lord, I hope I love California enough to die for it, but I have seven children. I can't die. I need you to confirm this to me."

Isaiah 53 reveals that Christ made intercession at the cross. True intercession puts you on death ground, and there principalities of Satan are broken. Jesus destroyed the works of the devil at the cross.

I flew to San Francisco to mobilize and then returned to Los Angeles. I began to fast. On the morning of my 50th birthday I met with a young man who happened to be married to the Peruvian woman who had earlier seen the Minerva dream. Without knowing anything of the beginnings of my fast, he said, "My wife just had another dream last night. A woman came to her and said, 'Lou is fasting the fast you dreamed about three years ago. He thinks he's going to die, but he will not die!'" I sat in shock and awe. Suddenly, I was catapulted from the thought that this might only be a good idea to knowing that this was a divine commission from heaven! Faith was born in my heart because I knew this was God's chosen fast. My ears were opened, and I set my face to obey the heavenly vision.

Now, I understood that Minerva was the Roman counterpart to the Canaanite goddess Ashtoreth mentioned in the Bible, where she represents the demonic principality that gave power to Queen Jezebel. In Revelation 2, the angel of the church of Thyatira declared,

> These things says the Son of God, who has eyes like a flame of fire, and His feet like fine brass: "I know your works, love, service, faith, and your patience; and as for your works, the last are more than the first. Nevertheless, I have a few things against you, because you allow that woman Jezebel, who calls herself a prophetess, to teach and seduce My servants to commit sexual immorality and eat things sacrificed to idols. And I gave her time to repent of her sexual immorality, and she did not repent. Indeed I will cast her into a sickbed, and those who commit adultery with her into great tribulation, unless they repent of their deeds. I will kill her children with death, and all the churches shall know that I am He who searches the minds and hearts. And I will give to each one of you according to your works . . . He who overcomes, and keeps My works until the end, to him I will give power over the nations." (Rev. 2:18-23, 26)

God was searching the hearts and minds of the church in

Thyatira, not just its outward actions. Jesus, whose eyes are blazing with fire and his feet with burnished bronze, is the jealous God who will brook no rivals to the fires of His love. In this passage in Revelation 2, Jesus is describing the spiritual battle concerning sexual laxity facing the church at Thyatira. He speaks of judgment for tolerating this spirit but then declares that "He who overcomes this Jezebel spirit will be given authority over the nations." Reading this, I knew that I could not bind the spirit of Jezebel over California if that spirit bound me. I began my fast, repenting daily of inward toleration of Jezebel, the lust of the eyes, and any compromise. Every day I would see myself clothed in the robes of Christ's perfect righteousness. Then day by day I would take my stand in the spirit before that spirit of Jezebel (not a spirit about women but a demonic principality that holds sway over the nations) and say, "I declare the victory of the cross over the spirit of Jezebel in California!" I wasn't railing at the devil, I was standing in Christ's victory alone.

Now there are many questions regarding how we wage spiritual warfare. I wouldn't encourage my method or my spiritual posturing to everyone, but I was clearly led by the Holy Spirit to stand against that spirit in a forty-day water fast. This was the prayer strategy God gave me.

On the 31st day, after speaking on fasting in San Diego, I spent the night at Hotel Circle. At one o'clock in the morning, I dreamed possibly the most liberating and glorious dream of my life. In the dream, I was flying over California like a soaring eagle, roaring the victory of the cross over Jezebel! I woke out of the dream roaring and knew that in that very moment something had broken in the spirit realm, that in some measure Satan had been pushed back and Christ had taken ground in my state of California.

That morning I flew from San Diego to St. Louis. As I took off, looking out of my airplane window, I saw a big mural on the side of the airport terminal with the face of Charles Lindbergh painted on it. I hadn't known that the airport was called the Lindbergh Field. Charles Lindbergh, you may recall, was the young man who flew the first transatlantic flight from New York to Paris. He made history and was acclaimed as a worldwide hero. As I was flying to St. Louis, I had one of those moments in which I was vulnerable to grace. Fasting makes you vulnerable to moments of grace, moments of revelation, when you experience the kiss of God's intimacy. I heard the inward voice of the Lord say, "You are St. Louis to me, and you're flying The Spirit of St. Louis." Not fully knowing what it meant or the implications of the voice, I began to weep because I knew He was calling my name Louis and identifying my calling by the name of Lindbergh's plane, The Spirit of St. Louis.

My friend picked me up that morning in St. Louis and said, "Lou, I had a dream about you last night at three o'clock in the morning." Taking into account the time difference, he had seen the dream at the exact same time I had seen my dream. He said, "I heard a voice which said, 'Because Lou has been faithful on this fast, I have given him authority over Jezebel in the nations, and wherever TheCall goes I will establish my house of prayer.'" Once again I knew something had broken in the spirit, and the implications could be that when the Church enters into united extended fasting worldwide, that demonic spirit can be shaken in the nations across the globe!

Stirred by this whirlwind, I looked up Charles Lindbergh and found out that his plane, The Spirit of St. Louis, was built in San Diego and its first flight was from San Diego to St. Louis. I had no idea, but oh the wonder! I sensed the Lord speaking, "What Lindbergh did in the natural, you are going to raise up in the spiritual. I want you to raise up an army of men and women, spiritual long-distance flyers, who will go on extended fasts like Daniel in Daniel 10, for breakthroughs against spiritual powers like no other generation has."

After my friend told me his dream about gaining authority in the nations, I was amazed that the dream actually quoted Revelation 2, "He who overcomes . . . I will give power over the nations." Had I actually won a spiritual battle in that fast? Could it be that a united, global forty-day fast with tens of thousands engaged, will break principalities and powers over governmental leaders who are not merely tolerating Jezebel, but through law are empowering demonic spirits of sexual immorality and witchcraft?

Almost immediately I saw the fruit of that fast. I was mobilizing in Sacramento for TheCall San Francisco when a young man came up to me after my message and introduced himself. I didn't know him, but he said, "I heard you speak on dreams, and so I prayed that I would have a dream. That night I dreamed that I was in a stadium filled with people. In that stadium there was a platform where kings would decree the word of the Lord. In the dream, Lou, you were on that platform declaring the word of the Lord. The governor of California, at that time, a man named Gray Davis, was in the stands. He didn't want to, but he had to submit to every word you were speaking, Lou."

In the next three months after my fast, we held two stadium gatherings with thirty thousand people in each. Sandwiched between those two gatherings was a forty-day call for California to fast. Soon after TheCall San Francisco a recall was initiated in California and Governor Gray Davis was impeached from his office. He had been passing every Jezebel-inspired bill. We knew at that moment that something had shifted over California that manifested physically in a political removal. If we have understood this correctly, the implications are enormous. God can raise up kings and bring them down through the mighty, united fasting of the Church! Out of that fast were birthed prayer movements for the ending of abortion (child sacrifice to Baal) and for the salvation and transformation of a hundred thousand LGBTQ people (state-sanctioned sexual immorality), the very altars that Jezebel established to seduce a nation with righteous roots into an apostasy where only seven thousand had not bowed the knee to Baal.

Though thousands will be fasting during these forty-day seasons with different kinds of fasts, I believe there will be some, particularly leaders in the Body of Christ and Christians with a call like Daniel in high places of government, education, business, and law, who will actually do ten, twenty-one, and forty-day fasts on water. I believe they will do this to gain a position of spiritual authority over spiritual powers and find the same divine promotion that rested on Daniel.

What if tens of thousands around the globe united in the Lent period, March 1 through April 9? Could places like Somalia, Afghanistan, and Tibet open to the gospel? What if the leaders of nations promoting persecution of the Church would have encounters with God or be removed from office? The Book of Daniel certainly gives us hope to that end. At the age of 83, in Daniel 10, Daniel's fast of twenty-one days inaugurated war in the heavens. Archangels warred against hosts of spiritual wickedness resulting in the shift of the public policy of Persia to a favorable posture toward the Jewish people. The Prince of Persia, a high-ranking demonic archangel, was dislodged from his place of influence over the natural kings of Persia, enabling them to rule rightly. Has the Church ever consistently wielded this mighty weapon that Christ has put at her disposal? The time has come for us to unite and test the efficacy and power of the fast that inaugurates war in the heavens.

Breaking the Spell of Jezebel

Extended fasting can produce a breakthrough where other methods fail. Elijah's experience with the forty-day fast is a clear example of this. Elijah had just witnessed one of the most dramatic demonstrations of God's power, yet despite this incredible victory on Mount Carmel, Jezebel was still alive, ruling over and dominating the culture of the land. Furious about the death of her prophets and under the possession of the spirit of Ashtoreth, Jezebel cursed Elijah, vowing to kill the prophet.

At this point, some commentators believe that Elijah failed his calling, so the Lord was forced to raise another in his stead. No! It is my conviction that God used the curse of

Jezebel to reposition the lone prophet as a father to Elisha and Jehu to release a generational anointing that could alone defeat Baal.

The angel of the Lord found Elijah exhausted, on the verge of collapse, and suicidal. After cooking bread and feeding the prophet, the angel of the Lord said, "'Arise and eat, because the journey is too great for you.' So he arose, and ate and drank; and he went in the strength of that food forty days and forty nights as far as Horeb, the mountain of God" (1 Kings 19:7-8). Elijah returned to the same place where Moses, generations before, had fulfilled his own forty-day fast. I believe that the forty-day fast was an enactment of covenant renewal and an act of spiritual warfare against Jezebel's sorceries. The fast broke the curse of Jezebel, and still today the forty-day fast will help cleanse and deliver us from her witchcraft.

At one point, while contemplating the significance of a nationwide forty-day fast, I was surprised to read in Francis Frangipane's wonderful revelatory little book, *The Jezebel Spirit*, how in 1971 his church was led to do a forty-day fast to war against the witchcraft of Jezebel. Similarly, Richard Gazowsky, in his book, *The Prophetic Whisper*, shares the significance of a forty-day strategy that the Lord gave him to break the powers of darkness. While praying with his wife, looking over San Francisco Bay, concerning a woman they knew who was being tempted with adultery, a huge swarm of flies rose up from the waters as if to attack them. It was so bizarre that Gazowsky inquired of the Lord concerning this strange event. The Lord said,

> "I am going to show you a secret vulnerability in Satan's kingdom. His weakness is in the flies." Later that day, we went to the Carmel Public Library and looked up the word "fly". . . . I discovered that the meaning of Beelzebub, one of the names of Satan is, "Lord of the flies.". . . Scientists have discovered that flies have a reproductive period that lasts from four hours to over forty days, depending upon the species. When pest controllers go to eradicate flies in a certain area, they spray pesticides every day for a forty-day period. If they destroy the reproductive cycles of presently existing flies,

they can kill off a whole generation of future flies. *I then saw what God was trying to show me . . . if a Christian will pray consistently for a forty-day period, they will be able to conquer most of Satan's strongholds in their life.*

The RAF

A contending house of prayer must gain air supremacy over principalities and powers through extended fasting and prayer.

In July 2004, we gathered fifty young people from across the nation to Colorado Springs to fast and pray day and night for fifty days. God had given us a very clear prayer assignment to pray for the ending of abortion and the raising up of a pro-life president who would appoint pro-life judges. At the beginning of those fifty days, I taught them about Daniel's twenty-one-day fast, as described in Daniel 10.

As we have seen earlier, Daniel's fasting and prayer inaugurated a war in heaven between holy archangels and the demonic prince of Persia. This dark prince of Persia, an invisible demonic being, is found in this passage playing the puppet strings over the earthly kings of Persia, influencing them to promote anti-Semitic policies directed against the Jews. Daniel, being deeply concerned about the affairs of his people, set himself to pray and fast for understanding concerning the situation.

After twenty-one days of spiritual battle, a mighty archangel from heaven, with the help of Michael, the angelic prince over Israel, dislodged the demonic prince of Persia from its position of spiritual influence over the human kings of Persia. The archangel then came to Daniel with a message from heaven:

> Do not fear, Daniel, for from the first day that you set your heart to understand, and to humble yourself before your God, your words were heard; and I have come because of your words. But the prince of the kingdom of Persia withstood me twenty-one days; and behold, Michael, one of the chief princes, came to help me, for I had been left alone there with the kings of Persia (Dan. 10:12-13).

Some key commentators say that the words, "For I had been left alone there with the kings of Persia," should be better translated, "and I remained there (as victorious on a field of battle) over the kings of Persia." Daniel's fasting, in cooperation with the angelic movement, shifted the public policy of the kings of Persia in favor of the Jews.

After teaching on Daniel 10, I exhorted those young people with the declaration, "You are the RAF—the Royal Air Force. Winston Churchill said of the RAF during the Battle for Britain, 'Never has so much been owed by so many to so few.' You must win the spiritual battle over the elections through fasting and prayer like Daniel won his victory. You will know if you won the spiritual battle in the heavens during this time of intensive prayer if a pro-life president is elected, and you will know if you lost if a pro-choice president is elected. It is your responsibility along with all the saints who are praying in America to prevail in prayer over this election for the sake of the thousands of unborn children that this election will affect."

The RAF was the Royal Air Force of Great Britain. When Hitler had swept across Europe with his lightning-fast military machine, crushing every foe and finally compelling France to surrender, the main barrier to a complete European takeover was the British Isles. Hitler set his sights on the military subjugation of the great people of these isles.

To take these islands, it was necessary for the Luftwaffe, the German Air Force, to gain air supremacy and destroy the Royal Air Force. With the destruction of the RAF complete, nothing could restrain the war machine of Germany from sweeping over Great Britain.

It was in this defining moment of history that the RAF, outnumbered and outgunned, hurled itself against the superior forces of the Luftwaffe. Day after day and week after week, with hundreds of its courageous pilots being killed, the RAF continued to withstand the great air assault. The German forces could not gain air superiority and finally withdrew from their military objective of destroying the United Kingdom.

Prime Minister Winston Churchill was so moved by the RAF's outrageous and sacrificial stand that he uttered to General Ismay, "Don't speak to me. I have never been so moved." After a few minutes, he leaned forward and said, "Never in the field of human conflict has so much been owed by so many to so few." Before this great battle Churchill had declared, "The Battle of Britain is about to begin. Members of the Royal Air Force, the fate of generations lies in your hands." I had essentially said the same things to these young people, "The future of America is in your hands. You must gain air supremacy in these elections."

On the 47th evening of continuous day and night worship and prayer, I met David Manuel for the first time. He is the co-author of a trilogy of brilliant books on the providential history of America. I told him nothing about my RAF prophecy and asked him to speak that night to those young people. At the end of his message, he suddenly kicked in to what I knew was the prophetic word. He said to those young intercessors, "You are the RAF! Never has so much been owed by so many to so few!" You could feel and almost hear the gasp of amazement that reverberated across the room. Those young people knew that heaven had heard and history was being made. A pro-life president was elected, two pro-life judges were appointed, and now Roe v. Wade, the landmark 1973 court case legalizing abortion, is being sieged from every side.

God has given me a life mandate: to raise up a generation who will give themselves to extended fasting and prayer for breakthroughs against the spiritual forces of wickedness in the heavenly places. The last days generation, as described in Revelation 12, will so command air supremacy that Satan will lose his position in heaven and be cast down to the earth because he will not be strong enough to resist any longer. Once again the voice of Jesus will be heard in every place where darkness and injustice boasts of its dominion, saying, "I saw Satan fall like lightning."

CHAPTER 8

THE FREEDOM FAST

Then the disciples came to Jesus privately and said, "Why could we not cast it out?" So Jesus said to them, "Because of your unbelief . . . This kind does not go out except by prayer and fasting."
Matt. 17:19-21

In 2003, prior to TheCall at the Rose Bowl in Pasadena, I was mobilizing Hispanic pastors and young leaders. After the meeting, a young Hispanic youth leader came up to me and said that he'd never heard of TheCall before but the name of his ministry was The Call. He had received it one night through a dream. In the dream he saw young people falling into these devastating and destructive fires and waters. The fires were sexual immorality and deep perversion. The waters were brooding and swirling with death. He saw suicide, drugs, witchcraft, and the cords of death destroying these precious lives. The scene was so dark that he found himself trying to claw his way out of the dream. As he was scrambling to get out, he heard an audible voice, "The answers to this darkness will only be found in Matthew 17." Eventually, he fell back to sleep and dreamed exactly the same dream with hearing the same audible voice, "The answer to this darkness will only be found in Matthew 17." A third time he dreamed that same dream followed by that same message. Upon waking up after the third dream, he immediately turned to Matthew 17. The young man was stunned beyond amazement. He found that Matthew 17 was the story of how a father's son was possessed by a demon who threw the boy into the fires and into the waters. The disciples could not cast the demon out. Jesus rebuked the demon and delivered the boy. When asked by His disciples why they could not cast it out, Jesus replied, "Because of your unbelief . . . this kind does not go out except by prayer and fasting" (Matt. 17:20-21).

I was blown away by the graphic nature of this young man's dream in so accurately depicting the spiritual reality of Matthew 17. As I pondered this young man's encounter, I was drawn to the beginning of the chapter. The chapter begins with the transfiguration of Jesus with Elijah and Moses on the mountain. All three men fasted for forty days. Moses fasted for forty days, saw the glory of God, and delivered a whole nation from the demons of Egypt. Elijah fasted for forty days, broke the power of Jezebel's witchcraft, and then anointed the next generation with a double portion of his prophetic spirit. Baal worship was brought low and the altar of Baal became a latrine. Jesus fasted for forty days and broke the power of Satan Himself and through His death and resurrection destroyed the works of the devil. Through prayer and fasting, we too will cast the powers of death out of a generation!

It is more than interesting to me that the only recorded fast that Jesus ever did was a forty-day fast. Could it be that the global forty-day fast will begin to shatter the powers of death, sickness, disease, and sexual insanity over the coming generation?

The second fast I remember doing in my life was a ten-day fast, praying with my friend for the power to deliver people from demonic oppression. For ten days we fasted, praying for one thing: the anointing to cast out demons. On the tenth day my pastor Che Ahn called me and said, "Come and pray with me for a person that needs freedom." I went with him.

Suddenly, in the midst of our praying for this young woman, demons began to manifest violently. In that same moment, the power of God broke into that room, as we commanded that spirit to leave. It was an almost instantaneous deliverance! For weeks demons would manifest and be cast out as we prayed for others. I realized that extended fasting is a key to mighty deliverance power! Will not the Church wield this mighty weapon where darkness fills the earth?

If our Master fasted for forty days, overcame Satan, and delivered the captives, should not the Church with one mighty unified assault on the citadel of hell avail itself of such a weapon? It is time for apostolic methodology for apostolic power!

Stevie's Story

In his excellent book, *The Hidden Power of Prayer and Fasting*, Mahesh Chavda tells a moving story about touching a broken child through prayer and fasting. It is another example of the power of fasting and prayer to release captives from the power of darkness. At the time, Mahesh was working at a hospital for mentally handicapped children in Lubbock, Texas.

I'll never forget the day I met a 16-year-old boy whom I'll call "Stevie". Stevie was a victim of Down's Syndrome, a moderate to severe form of mental retardation often characterized by reduced mental capacity and certain physical deformities. Stevie was afflicted with something even worse. He was a self-mutilator who was driven to cry out and beat himself in the face constantly.

The staff psychologist at the school had secured permission from state officials in Austin, Texas to administer electric shock therapy to Stevie for a six-month period . . . administering electric shocks any time he beat himself. He just got worse and worse instead of better. By the time I was there, his face felt like dry alligator skin because he beat himself continuously.

Finally, the attendants tied Stevie's hands in splints so that he couldn't bend his arms to reach his face. The only problem was that the other children in his dormitory ward developed a new game once they figured out that Stevie's hands were bound at his sides. They liked to run up behind him and push him so hard that he would lose his balance and fall down. Since Stevie could no longer instinctively shield his face with his arms because of the splints, every time the kids on the ward played their game and pushed him, Stevie would land facedown on the floor without any way to protect himself or soften the landing. Most of the time we would find him with blood streaming from his nose, lips, and mouth. Whenever I would come, Stevie could sense God's love coming from me and he would put his head on my shoulder and just weep.

Finally I said, "Lord, You told me that You sent me here to love these children. What is the answer for Stevie?" Very clearly I heard the voice of the Holy Spirit say, "This kind goes not out but by prayer and fasting." Although this may be a very familiar scripture to you, it sounded totally foreign to me. I had attended a Bible university for four years and had earned my Bachelor's Degree there, but I didn't even know that the Spirit was quoting a scripture passage to me from Matthew 17:21!

Another thing I'd failed to learn during my four years of Bible school training was the subject of fasting. I said, "Fasting—doesn't that mean no food and no water?" So I didn't eat and didn't drink water or Coke or anything else for that matter. I was also unaware of the fact that when you do without water, your priorities will change. By the third day of my fast without water, I began to get jealous every time I heard someone washing their hands in a bathroom sink!

On the fourth day the Lord spoke to me and said, "You can drink," so I started drinking water. But I did not break the fast until the fourteenth day and the Lord said, "Now pray for Stevie." When I arrived for my shift at the school that day, I took Stevie into my little office cubicle and said, "Stevie, I know your mind may not understand what I'm saying, but your spirit is eternal. I want to tell you that I am a servant of the Lord Jesus Christ. I've come to preach good news to you. I want you to know that Jesus Christ came to set the captives free."

Then I said, "In the name of Jesus, you evil spirit of mutilation, you let him go now in the name of Jesus." Suddenly Stevie's body was flung about eight feet away from me and hit the other wall of the cubicle! When Stevie hit the wall, his body was elevated about three feet above the floor, and then he slid down to the floor and let out a long sigh. Immediately, I smelled an incredibly foul smell of rotten eggs and burning sulfur in the room, which gradually faded away.

I quickly went to Stevie, cradled him in my arms, and removed his splints while he watched with wide eyes. Then Stevie began to bend his arms and gently feel his face. I watched him softly touch his eyes, his nose, and his ears; then he started sobbing. He had realized that for the first time he was not being driven to beat himself. He was gently touching his face and he had been delivered! In that unforgettable moment, the Lord revealed to me what a powerful weapon He has given to us to pull down strongholds and set the captives free. Within a few months, all the scabs had fallen off of Stevie's face. He had begun to heal because he had stopped beating himself.

Years ago, I was speaking on the marriage between a man and a woman only. Suddenly, a young man struggling to be free from the same-sex desire stood and interrupted me with this challenge: "You have no right to tell the LGBTQ community they cannot have their civil rights unless you can bring them the true freedom the gospel promises!" I felt it was a rebuke to me and the Church. Maybe the bills being passed and the judicial decisions being made that are threatening our religious liberties are happening because we have not manifested the delivering power of Jesus for those longing to be free. Recently on a long fast, I saw in a dream a message delivered on ticker tape that read, "You said you would deliver us 418." Upon waking, it was like I could hear the groaning of those crying for freedom and demanding a new unrolling of the scroll of Jesus in Luke 4:17-18.

> And the scroll of the prophet Isaiah was handed to him. Unrolling it, he found the place where it is written: "The Spirit of the Lord is on me, because he has anointed me to proclaim good news to the poor. He has sent me to proclaim freedom for the prisoners and recovery of sight for the blind, to set the oppressed free."

The unrolling of the scroll of Jesus was preceded by His forty-day fast. It is time once again for a new manifestation of Luke 4:18 on earth. Those bound in darkness demand it! It is time to enter into the Jesus Fast in order to gain the spiritual authority necessary to set people free.

Arthur Wallis, in his significant book, *God's Chosen Fast*, tells the story of a man in China who was delivered from opium addiction. He fasted so much that he gained a place of spiritual authority. No demon of opium addiction could stand before him. People came from all over to be set free. He changed his name to Sheng Mo, meaning the Conqueror of Demons. God, once again, raise up a generation through fasting and prayer that could call itself the Conqueror of Demons!

CHAPTER 9

THE FAST TO UNROLL YOUR SCROLL

So many of our dreams are messages from heaven, but we have been taught that dreams are mere psychobabble or just meaningless thoughts springing from some subconscious mist deep within us. No! Dreams are the last days language of the Holy Spirit.

Imagine that in your youth you had seen a dream, a vision, or heard God's voice unveiling His divine destiny for your life. Suppose a night vision came to you showing you your pathway and your purpose, a guiding constellation lighting up your highway of commanding destiny. Instead of thrashing about in life in frustration, uncertainty, and confusion, you would have discovered a sort of blueprint, a navigational chart for your life journey. Instead of unceasingly exploring career fairs, taking career personality assessments, or switching from job to job, you would live with a deep, joyful confidence and peaceful assurance, because in the dream you had received God's official signet ring of sonship and calling. Even better, you woke in awe that the Holy Spirit and your guardian angels were now with you to assist in your journey and even be the guarantors of the vision's wonderful future and fulfillment.

Maybe this is what happened in your life. If so, that is amazing! But for most people, this is not the case. For most of us, we all go through the same process of trying to find ourselves. We talk to parents, family friends, and admissions counselors who give us their best guess as to what we will be good at and what will make us prosper. We get fast-tracked into programs based on external values and social structures doomed to fail. These programs are created to lead us to careers that will allow us to buy houses, have kids, and create retirement nest eggs to maybe one day retire in some comfortable haven or exotic dwelling. While this "assembly line" purpose-finding has good intentions and may be helpful, it also has a built-in futility. Because these plans are created externally, they are inherently devoid of the supernatural and circumvent the custom-made plan the Author and Finisher of our life story has envisioned for us before we were even conceived.

The value system created by these objective road maps of success will inevitably lead to futility and disappointment by the end of our lives. Yet, for lack of another perceived option, this is how most of us live. Friends, God has a better way! I call this better way, "Unroll your scroll through the *vision quest!*"

In 1999, I prayed the prayer, "How can I turn America back to God?" It became the defining prayer of my entire life. God answered that prayer when a woman came to me and said, "You don't know me but the Lord told me to pay your salary this year because you are going to start something with the youth of America in prayer that will help turn the nation back to God." She paid my salary for fifteen years and birthed the movement of TheCall.

Some months after she first spoke to me, I had a dream where I was overwhelmed with the impossibility of seeing America turn back to God. In the dream, a scroll rolled down before me with the scripture Luke 1:17 written on it. I read these words written on the scroll, "He will go on before the Lord in the spirit and power of Elijah to turn the hearts of the fathers to the children and the rebellious to the wisdom of the righteous." When I woke up, the Lord spoke to me, ""What I am pouring out in America is stronger than the rebellion!" At that moment, I knew that Luke 1:17 was the scroll that God had written with TheCall included in it. I believe that God wrote in His book that TheCall would be a John the Baptist-type movement that would help to prepare the way of the Lord's coming to America in a great revival. For the last two decades, we have gathered hundreds of thousands in fields, arenas, and stadiums to fast and pray, believing that it would lead to a moment when, like John the Baptist, we would declare, "Behold! The Lamb of God who takes away the sin of the world" (John 1:29)! Then, the Luke 4:18 scroll of Jesus would be unrolled.

In this life-altering destiny dream, God showed me His intention for my life and ministry as I read the scroll that unrolled before me. David said in Ps. 40:6-7,

> Sacrifice and offering You did not desire; my ears You have opened . . . Then I said, "Behold, I come; in the scroll of the book it is written of me. I delight to do Your will, O my God."

When David's ears were opened, when he by revelation discovered what God had written in his destiny scroll before he was conceived, then he could proclaim, "Behold, I come!" This is not arrogance. This is sonship! He knew who he was, and he could step boldly into the earth to do the will of his Father.

Likewise, God opened my ears in the Luke 1:17 dream that showed me my scroll. Knowing the days my Heavenly Father had ordained for me, I could confidently step into the world and say, "Behold, I come!" This encounter became an anchor for my life and has enabled me to persevere and continue to believe God in faith whether I encounter sunny days or am driven by a tempest like the disciples.

I cannot overstate the value of receiving a revelatory scripture, a divine dream, or guiding vision for your life. So many times people say, "It was just a dream." Just a dream? Who knows what a messenger from heaven had to fight through to deliver that message. So many of our dreams are messages from heaven, but we have been taught that dreams are mere psychobabble or just meaningless thoughts springing from some subconscious mist deep within us. No! Dreams are the last days language of the Holy Spirit.

> And it shall come to pass in the last days, says God, that I will pour out of My Spirit on all flesh . . . your young men shall see visions, your old men shall dream dreams (Acts 2:17).

There must be a rejection of cynicism and a recovery of the sense of the sacred when speaking of dream communication. Yes, let us always test a dream to see if it aligns with and does not contradict Scripture, but let us not rob ourselves or our children of a genuine encounter with the Holy Spirit just because our spiritual lenses have been blurred or cracked by a Western materialistic worldview instead of being supernaturally enlightened by a biblical worldview.

A beneficent heaven would not turn away anyone on a vision quest seeking to know heaven's customized plan for their lives. Those who go into the wilderness of fasting and praying, forsaking all for this pearl of great price, will not be disappointed.

> How much more will your Father who is in heaven give good gifts to those who ask Him? (Matt. 7:11)

Even the Native Americans, unaware of the life-saving grace found in Jesus Christ, knew the value of life-defining dreams. Young men, striving to become warriors, would venture into the wilderness and fast for days in order to receive some type of spiritual encounter that would guide their lives. The Lakota Tribe had a song that went like this:

> You cannot harm me, you cannot harm one, who has dreamed a dream like mine.

While their search was misguided, as they were without Christ, they knew that to receive a spiritual experience and vocational dream guidance through fasting would give a greater purpose for their lives. We in the West have thrown away the keys that other religions have used to unlock spiritual secrets, though we must remember that revelation apart from Christ leads to deception and darkness. Millions of Muslims fast during the month of Ramadan; on the 28th night they call on Allah to give them dreams of their destiny. They call that night the Night of Power, or the Night of Destiny. Many have encounters and many have visitations from Jesus, the man dressed in white. While much of the Church dismisses this form of revelation as deception and superstition, the Muslim culture is closer to the Eastern culture of the Bible than the Western culture of modernism and naturalism. We need to recover the Eastern mindset of the Hebrews, who believed that God spoke to them in dreams and visions.

> Your eyes saw my substance, being yet unformed. And in Your book they all were written, the days fashioned for me, when as yet there were none of them. (Psalm 139:16)

God knew David before he even existed, and He knew you too! Furthermore, God has a book where He has written down His plan for each and every day of your life. This book was written about you before you even stepped foot on this planet. Even the very work of our lives was prepared for us by the Lord, as shown in Eph. 2:10.

> For we are His workmanship, created in Christ Jesus for good works, which God prepared beforehand that we should walk in them.

So how do you find your scroll and what God has written in it? How do you unlock God's divine plan for your life that was custom-made for you only? Luke 4 is God's prototype blueprint for a man or woman to find and walk into their destiny. Jesus was baptized at the Jordan River and was immediately led by the Spirit into the wilderness to fast for forty days. He came out of the fast in the power of the Spirit, preaching with powerful signs and wonders following. He was fulfilling the very scroll written about Him in Isaiah 61.

His is the prototype for the unfolding of your own scroll! Be baptized in the love of God and hear His voice that you are His beloved son! Then go to the wilderness in extended fasting. Seek God's face and go on a vision quest. Ask earnestly for your Heavenly Father to unroll your scroll. Ask for dreams, devour the Scriptures, and then walk out the Word and those visions in careful obedience to the voice of the Lord. Extended fasting opened up Jesus' scroll, and it is one of God's prescribed methods for unrolling your scroll, that which has already been written in heaven about you.

In 2018, on the Central Coast of California, a new scroll began to unfold before me, not my scroll, but the scroll of the great deliverer, Jesus. Many across California had been fasting for forty days. We were at the Healing Rooms in Santa Maria where we were ending the fast on April 9. At that time, my intercessory friend Paul Amabile had a dream in which I was tightening my belt ten notches. In the dream I was asking if anyone was willing to extend the fast ten more days.

Paul Cain lived in Santa Maria, and when we met with him he spoke of the prophecy by his mother Anna Cain. She told her son Paul that the Lord had one last prophetic word to give him before she died. She said that it would be the most important prophecy she would ever give to her son and the whole world. Then she slipped into a coma. Weeks passed. Suddenly, one night Anna woke from the coma to say, "Paul, the Lord is going to release over your life and the Body of Christ across the world—Luke 4:18." After prophesying, she slipped back into a coma and then passed away. My friend Mike Bickle, who was there with Paul, noted that she passed on 4/18 at 4:18 PM. We realized that the ten days of the tightening of the belt beginning on April 9 would end on April 18, 4/18. For ten days, hundreds gathered, praying for the Luke 4:18 scroll of Jesus to be unrolled over the whole earth.

It's time! Would you begin to pray for the full manifestation of the Luke 4:18 scroll of Jesus on earth?

The first scroll the Lord gave me was the John the Baptist scroll of Luke 1:17. After twenty years of fasting and praying for that scroll to be fulfilled with TheCall, I am now constrained to give the next twenty years of my life, God willing, to fast and pray for the manifestation of Jesus' scroll —Luke 4:18. If I saw the fulfillment of the first scroll in such measure, why shouldn't I believe that I will see the fulfillment of the second scroll? For the last words of John were not "Prepare the way of the Lord," but "Behold! The Lamb of God who takes away the sin of the world!" If Jesus' scroll is ever released in fullness to the earth, then no mental illness will stand before the Church. Addictions and demons will flee and every sickness and disease will be healed. Cities will be shaken. Let the Church worldwide fast for the unrolling of the Jesus scroll!

Extended fasts have long been the landing strip for destiny revelation in my life. I have found that in the scroll God wrote about me, dreams have been like chapter titles pointing out my future. These dreams have become navigational charts for my future course settings. Dreams are like the spies who spied out the Promised Land for forty days prior to the Israelites entering. In extended fasting, even for forty days, God can show you your promised land through destiny dreams. I encourage you during your fast to cry out to God for the unrolling of your scroll and that He would give you dreams to reveal to you your purpose! You have entered the most exciting adventure of your life. You are on a *vision quest*!

CHAPTER 10

THE FAST OF GENERATIONAL TRANSFER

We've taught our children to feast and play; the times demand they fast and pray!

The forty-day fast is meant to turn us back to the original place of covenant. Not only did the forty-day fast of Elijah break the power of Jezebel's intimidation and influence, more importantly, it prepared him to receive the most important commission of his life: to anoint Elisha. Whereas before, the Lord was in the fire at Mount Carmel, now on the mountain "the Lord was not in the fire." He was in the still, small, prophetic whisper. We have to understand that our battles and our victories or defeats are multigenerational. Without Elisha, the double portion son, Elijah's commission to turn the nation back to God and rid the land of Baal worship remained unfinished. Sons and daughters finish the work of their fathers. Here is where we've missed it before. The fast burn of revival is not enough. One generation receives the outpouring of revival but loses it in the next generation. We must have the quick burn of revival and the slow burn of fathering the next generation. Between the fire and the fathering is Elijah's forty-day fast. I don't believe the revival we long for will come in

America without extended fasting. It is interesting that Moses fasted for forty days and had a spiritual son named Joshua, which means "the Lord is salvation." Elijah fasted for forty days and fathered a double portion son, Elisha, which means "the Lord saves." And John the Baptist fasted throughout his life and prepared the way for the greatest double portion Son, Jesus, which means "the Lord is salvation." Could it be that the forty-day fast will produce a generation of double portion evangelists that will reap the worldwide harvest?

In the case of John and Jesus, both the spiritual father and the double portion son fasted for forty days. This pattern holds true in our day as well. Franklin Hall's fast directly preceded the release of the great sons of evangelism: Billy Graham, T.L. Osborn, and many others. Even in my life I have watched the effect of Bill Bright's fast in raising up sons and daughters who are now being greatly used by God. The forty-day fast is a key to uncaging and releasing the great evangelists.

In calling you and the globe to this fast, a part of my purpose is to call two generations to a forty-day season of fasting from food (according to each person's ability) and from television, computer games, and social media, to cleanse ourselves from the effects of the spirit that seduces us into sexual immorality, greed, entertainment addiction, and spiritual malaise.

What would happen in the nations if for forty days we sealed the electronic cultural sewer that flows nightly into our living rooms, through our cell phones and iPads, to spend our strength seeking the Lord? What if tens of thousands of spiritual fathers and mothers across our nation fasted for forty days, repenting and cleansing themselves of all inward toleration of sexual immorality, addiction to food and entertainment, closing the windows of hell in their homes? Let these parents pray daily for forty days for their spiritual and physical children to break off rebellion and for deliverance from addictions, freedom from demons, healing for disabilities, and hope for the depressed and suicidal.

What would happen if a young generation of Elishas would fast for forty days to be cleansed from lust, TV addiction, pornography, spiritual mediocrity, and rebellion against their parents, believing for a double portion of the Holy Spirit to rest on their lives?

I was privileged to experience the power of this principle of bi-generational fasting and generational transfer with my own son Jesse. I can tell you that it works!

Jesse's Story

"America is receiving her apostles, prophets, and evangelists, but it has not yet seen her Nazirites!" These audible thundering words shook me from my sleep at four o'clock in the morning in January 2000. It was God. It was a promise. It was His explosive response to the heart hunger of a 13-year-old's desire to be completely separated to God. That young man was my son Jesse. That evening he had come to me fervently expressing his desire to be a Nazirite until TheCall DC, a massive prayer gathering that would take place later that year in September. He told me that he didn't want to cut his hair until TheCall. He wanted to fast for forty days on juice and smoothies. He was determined that, following the fast, he would not eat meat or sweets until TheCall. He said, "Dad, I don't want to play baseball this year,"—he was the best pitcher on the team—"all that I want to do is run with you, Dad, and pray for revival in America."

I went to bed that night pondering what response I should give to such an extreme request. I didn't have to ponder long. God responded to me. It was almost as if He couldn't contain Himself. He couldn't wait for the morning dawn to give His own response. He was looking for someone. He was hotly pursuing a completely abandoned heart upon which He could send His holy fire. He had found His Nazirite.

Jesse and I fasted for forty days together. Eight months later on September 2, 2000, at TheCall DC, when 400,000 young people gathered in Washington, D.C., not for a festival, but for a fast, Jesse stood on that great stage and cried out to God for the Nazirites to arise in America. When he prayed, it was as if his words gave articulation to what was already subterraneously rumbling beneath the soul-surface of a whole new generation. When he cried out, "Release the Nazirites, let the long-hairs arise!", it was as if a volcanic eruption occurred. His prayer released a roar on the National Mall, and the video of that prayer leaked to the Philippines, where it catalyzed 150,000 Filipinos to gather to fast and pray! It spread throughout Southeast Asia and touched the world. I believe that when Jesse and I fasted together on a multigenerational fast, it became the catalyst for a move of God in America and beyond. Let Elijah rise to once again stretch himself out in prayer to raise a generation from the dead. Let Elijah fast for forty days and anoint a generation of double portion sons and daughters for the last days work to be accomplished. The whole earth is groaning for the manifestation of the sons of God. And just like Jesus was manifested as the Son of God out of the forty-day fast, so shall a generation of the sons of God be manifested through the forty-day fast.

CHAPTER 11

YOU CAN CLIMB THIS MOUNTAIN!

The opportunity of a lifetime must be seized within the lifetime of the opportunity.

Leonard Ravenhill

Recently, the wife of the young man who helped me write and edit this book had a dream in which they were struggling to climb a mountain that was very difficult and steep. She looked up and saw me above them on the mountain, calling and encouraging them to come up to the top of the mountain. This young man had been feeling a desire to fast. I said to him, "I think the mountain is the Mountain of the Lord. Moses fasted for forty days on the Mountain of the Lord and Elijah fasted for forty days on that same mountain. I think the Lord wants you to come up to the Mountain of the Lord and fast for forty days." He had just completed his water and juice fast at the time we were finishing this book. God has changed his life. He has discovered his scroll. The forty-day fast can be done and the rewards are very great.

Many reading this book may be stirred to enter into the forty days but are daunted by the sheer height of such a climbing endeavor. I understand. Paul boasted that he spoke in tongues more than you all. My claim to fame is that I've broken more fasts than you all. It is amazing that the minute you begin to fast, that beautiful pink box of donuts appears at the office, and, immediately, you start thinking, "I'll start my fast at Noon."

One time I was fasting, but after three days I became so weary of the fast. There in my kitchen (stay away from the kitchen while fasting) I looked both ways to see if my wife was watching, then secretly ate yogurt and chips. It tasted so good! Anything tastes good when you're fasting. The following day I was sitting in our house of prayer in Pasadena when a prophetic intercessor lady—a scary lady!—walked in. She saw me and said, "I had a dream about you last night, and in the dream you were sitting right where you're sitting now." I thought, "How wonderful! God knows my address!" Then she continued, "But in the dream I was very disappointed with you because you were supposed to be fasting but you were eating yogurt and chips!" Suddenly, I had fresh motivation to fast. Crazy! You're probably laughing hysterically or in shock. I was in shock. I'm not sure if God was playing with me, saying, "I'm watching you!" or if He was speaking to me soberly concerning my calling and commitment to treat fasting very seriously because of the great implications of it all. Probably the latter may be closer to the truth, but in the experience I felt the loving and grace-filled gaze of God.

I share this with you to dismantle any myths that I or anyone else is a spiritual superhero. There are some, I'm sure. But I'm like you. Extended fasting is not just for the 'Man of God' but for all us normal saints. We all struggle with the flesh. So often I've faltered in a fast and beaten myself up with shame. Don't go there. God loves the fact that you desire to fast. Your little "Yes" moves His heart. If you falter, get up and press on with a faith-filled heart. The face of heaven shines on you. And if you continue to falter, maybe the grace just isn't there. Eat and drink, knowing that you can never earn God's love. It is free and wonderful. Whether in fasting or feasting, do it in faith unto the Lord. There is no failure in fasting. Fasting is not about how well you did, but did you break through into faith? On a recent extended fast, I could not sustain it on water. I ate a little food each day. But on the final day, God broke through in an amazing way and gave me His blueprint for my next season. Faith came.

I'm not diminishing the call to be radical in your subjection of the flesh. Jesus did not succumb to temptation. I simply want to keep you from the pit of condemnation. Jesus was crucified between two thieves. On one side, there is the danger of demonic, pharisaical pride because you fasted so long and well. On the other side, Satan rises up and accuses you for your failure. Stay on the cross—in the center of God's truth and grace. I do want to encourage you by telling that there is a grace of fasting, when heaven has moved you and released a divine enabling to fast. I would encourage you to ask for this grace, the spirit of grace and supplication.

One young man came to me and said, "I have never fasted before, but when I heard you preach on this subject, my heart burned with faith. Pray for me that I would receive the grace to fast for forty days on water. I simply prayed, "Lord, release the grace on this man for the Jesus Fast." He came to me later and said, "Lou, it was amazing! I literally could not eat for forty days. Heaven was so real!" He did three different forty-day fasts in the next year and a half. On the last one he came to me saying that he had seen the dead raised! Oh God, release the grace of fasting over this reader and over the earth!

I would not encourage all to do forty-day water fasts. In fact, I insist that you be led by the Holy Spirit. Some who have not fasted wisely, or have broken their fasts too quickly, have hurt themselves. Some may want to go into shorter fasts of three, ten, or twenty-one days. Water is the fasting man's best friend because true hunger fades when you fast on water, and weakness drives you to God. On the other hand, juice fasts and Daniel Fasts continue to keep the hunger drive alive. Water kills it for a season. The benefit of a partial fast (not water fast) is that you can enjoy the pleasure and reward of fasting and still have the strength to work and carry on with normal activities. I've always found it helpful to fast with another brother, for "Two are better than one . . . for if they fall, one will lift up his companion" (Eccl. 4:9-10).

Have clear prayer goals for your fast. These goals must have a powerful hold over you. In fact, they must be more powerful than your hunger. Without a vision, people are unrestrained. I cannot restrain my hunger without a stronger prophetic promise that motivates my soul and dominates my flesh. Job said, "I have treasured the words of His mouth more than my necessary food" (Job 23:12).

Separate yourself from the influences of movies, television, social media, video games, and gossiping for forty days. Be a man or a woman of one thing; be all in, let there be no side issues, no distractions. You're seeking to move heaven and resist devils.

Join the global fasting community online at **thejesusfast.com** for daily devotionals and testimonies to encourage and stir your heart.

I would encourage you to write down three or four personal and prophetic focuses for your fast. You will be amazed down the road as you look back through the rearview mirror how those promises will have been fulfilled.

If you are joining the global Jesus Fast, I would suggest to pray along the following focal points for agreement:

1. For bridal love to fill the Church (Rev. 19:7)
2. A global manifestation of Jesus' evangelistic scroll (Luke 4:18)
3. The unity of the Body of Christ (John 17)
4. The global outpouring of the latter rain of revival (Joel 2:28)
5. Breakthroughs with your family and friends (Acts 16:31)
6. Laborers for the harvest (Matt. 9:38)
7. Unreached people groups (Matt. 24:14)
8. The salvation of Israel (Rom. 11:11-15).

The Reward of Fasting

> Moreover, when you fast, do not be like the hypocrites, with a sad countenance. For they disfigure their faces that they may appear to men to be fasting. Assuredly, I say to you, they have their reward. But you, when you fast, anoint your head and wash your face, so that you do not appear to men to be fasting, but to your Father who is in the secret place; and your Father who sees in secret will reward you openly. (Matt. 6:16-18)

Derek Prince wrote that every fast you do in faith and with a right heart will be rewarded. Jesus promises that when you fast in secret, the Father will reward you openly. You may not see the reward immediately, but the promise stands. I'm living in the open rewards of fasts I did thirty years ago. Many people ask, "Should we even tell people we are fasting since the Scriptures say we must fast in secret?" In the context of Matthew 5-7, Jesus is not speaking to the outward works of the disciples, but to their inward motivations. He is not saying that you shouldn't tell people you are fasting. He's going to the very heart of your motivations—why you are fasting. When you are fasting, it is right when you go to someone's house to tell them you are fasting, as otherwise they will offer you food and be offended because you don't want it. It is kindness. Many people use this scripture as an excuse not to fast, for fear that someone might know. That is not God's heart. Would it not please God that so many people were fasting that it would become normal to say, "I'm fasting today."? Then everyone will say, "Great! Then I get to eat your food!"

What is amazing about this passage as well is that Jesus uses the words, "when you fast" in two different ways. In the first, "you" is singular, speaking of when you fast individually. In the second, "you" is plural, speaking of when you as a people fast corporately. Jesus expected His disciples to fast individually in secret and corporately as a company. That fast is public! There is a great spiritual precedent and promised reward for both the individual fast and the corporate fast. I wonder what the reward will be when the Church worldwide joins in the "when you" (plural) fast.

Many books on fasting will give you practical advice in how to fast and how to break fasts, on the benefits and dangers of fasting, and the different types of fasts. This is not the objective of this book. This is a book for mobilization and for stirring faith for personal and worldwide breakthrough. This is a book inviting us to experience God's glory and love. This is a book of dreams and, if I may say so, God's dreams, dreams of a new world where Satan is cast down, where the Kingdom comes, where evangelism is easy, and where shouts of joy fill the streets because the Spirit of the Lord has come to heal every disease and sickness. This is a book about the Jesus Fast that will open the heavens and precipitate the latter rain. Let us all go up to the Mountain of the Lord! Let the earth go up in the global Jesus Fast.

Please go to **www.thejesusfast.global** to receive practical resources to help along in your fasting journey.

At the very moment we were finishing the last chapter of this book, this testimony came to us:

Great news! One of the objectives of my recent forty-day fast was to see my one-year-old daughter Victoria completely healed of arrhythmia and tachycardia. Today, we were given the news that her little heart is working perfectly. There is no need for more medicine or anything else! I am so thankful that my heart could explode!

OTHER BOOKS BY LOU ENGLE

A House That Contends by Lou Engle and Sam Cerny
A Moment to Confront by Lou Engle and Sam Cerny
Digging the Wells of Revival by Lou Engle and Tommy Tenney
Elijah's Revolution: Power, Passion and Commitment to Radical Change by Jim W. Goll, Lou Engle and Che H. Ahn
Fast Forward: A Call to Millennial Prayer Revolution by Lou Engle and Catherine Paine
Nazirite DNA by Lou Engle
Pray! Ekballo! by Lou Engle
The Call of the Elijah Revolution by James W. Goll and Lou Engle
The Call Revolution by Lou Engle and Che Ahn
The Jesus Fast: The Call to Awaken the Nations by Lou Engle, Dean Briggs, Bill Johnson and Daniel Kolenda

Lightning Source UK Ltd.
Milton Keynes UK
UKHW020615250420
362243UK00019B/1874